Letters to Erin

Letters to Erin

Calling a Generation of Young Women
to Give God Everything

Copyright © 2013
Rachel L. Thompson

OneWay Ministries
PO Box 2211
Naperville, IL 60567
web: www.owm.org
email: mail@owm.org

Letters to Erin is also available in electronic form using your favorite ebook reader.

Letters to Erin
ISBN: 978-0-9910892-7-7

Cover design by Jim Johanik and book design by Adara Haley, OneWay Studios, Aurora, Illinois
Printed in the United States of America

To Erin

Thank you for being the person God used to inspire this book. You were a beautiful bride the day I met you, but I've come to learn that you are even more beautiful on the inside.

Table of Contents

Introduction

My Story: The Life Behind the Letters

PART I: The Habits: Feeding Your Soul

PART II: The Heart: Reflecting Your God

PART III: The Home: Serving Your Family

On Being a Wife

Acknowledgements

First and foremost, thank You, Jesus, for being my Savior. You are truly a friend that sticks closer than a brother and I love You. You deserve all the credit for completing this good work You began in me.

Thank you, Michael, for your counsel, accountability and encouragement to press on. Without you, this book would have never been finished. I love doing life with you!

Thank you to our seven wonderful children—Hannah, Stephen, Esther, Sarah, David, Daniel and Rachel Joy—who went many a Thursday night without their mother so that I could write. You are each such a treasure to me!

Thanks to my dear friends, sisters, mother and mother-in-law who prayed for this project, read over the manuscript and gave helpful suggestions: Ruth, Annemarie, Sheri, Stephanie E., Laura, Heidi, Katie, Holly, Effie, Nadia, Stephanie H. and Katy. My life is immeasurably enriched by you all!

Thank you, Jim Johanik and Adara Haley, for your awesome work on the layout and cover design. You guys are a ton of fun and incredible coworkers in the gospel!

Preface

How These Letters Came to Be

Some days go by with little to mark them by way of special memory. Others remain fixed in our minds forever. July 23, 2005 was one such a day for me.

Michael and I were attending a family wedding in Colorado. As the couple beautifully committed their lives to each other, I was particularly struck by the bride, who, from the bottom of her heart, seemed determined to thrive in her roles as wife and Christ follower.

As I sat there during the ceremony, a thought hit me: so many young, Christian women stand in this place of new beginnings with all the potential and desire in the world. Yet they often lack an older woman or a fellowship of women to mentor them as they set out. Even many of those who have been walking with God for many years as wives and mothers still lack for this kind of advice and encouragement from others.

As I reflected on the wedding later that night, God impressed upon me that it was time for me to start writing down some of what He's taught me and share it, even with this new bride. It wasn't that I had the end-all answer to every issue she would ever face. And it certainly wasn't that I had arrived at a perfect place of wisdom and maturity myself. It was simply that His faithfulness had taken me a certain ways down the road and it was time to turn around and start passing something on.

Women mentoring women is not a new idea. It's something

that God actually thought of, and that He designed to be a part of the Christian life (Titus 2:3-5). We were not meant to grow alone, but in connection with other godly women from whom we could glean insights and inspiration. While this is often best done in person, God has also historically used written means to relay instruction and hope. Much of the New Testament, in fact, is comprised of letters written to teach and encourage fellow believers.

My overall prayer as I have written to Erin—and ultimately to her generation—stems from Ecclesiastes 12:11.

"The words of the wise are like goads, their collected sayings like firmly embedded nails–given by one Shepherd."

I have prayed that God would somehow take these "collected sayings" and use them, as a Shepherd uses a goad or a prod, to encourage women down His paths for them, while firmly embedding in their hearts truths born out of His Word. Ultimately, I've prayed that this collection of thoughts would reflect not my voice, but the voice of Jesus, the Great Shepherd Himself.

No matter if you are anticipating marriage and family someday, if you have been living it for many years, or if your once bustling house is now only occasionally graced by grandchildren, my hope and prayer is that something in the following pages would encourage your heart and possibly even inspire you to share with others your life and the lessons He's taught you.

It's simply one of the ways He wants to use us to reach the world for Him.

Rachel Thompson
Fall 2013

Dear Erin,

Welcome to the family!

I realize I hardly know you, so this may sound a little strange.
It's not every day, after all, that you get mail from a relative you've
only briefly met. The truth is that I feel compelled to write and share
some thoughts as you and Christopher begin your life together.

As you said your vows this past summer, something about your
heart struck me. I sensed in you a deep desire to be more than just
a normal wife, to be more than just an average Christian. And that
kind of desire is hard to forget.

Later that night as I was thinking about you, I felt a burden
to begin sharing with you some thoughts about life, marriage and
living for God with all your heart.

Believe me, I come at this with a great deal of humility because
I myself have so much yet to learn and so many areas where I still
need to grow! But I suppose if we all waited until we had arrived
at "perfect wisdom" before sharing our lives with others, godly
mentoring would never happen. So please know that this is the spirit
in which I write.

May God somehow use my words to build you up in your role
as Christopher's wife and Christ's servant. I pray that the letters to
come wouldn't just scratch the surface, but leave a deep imprint on
your heart by His Spirit. May He use them to give you direction,
counsel and wisdom to thrive in living the life He created you to
live.

So over the months and years ahead, and across the miles
between Chicago and Colorado, I hope you don't mind me pouring
out my heart to you.

With love,
Rachel

My Story:
the life behind the letters

- 1 -
grabbed by grace

He reached down from on high and took hold of me;
he drew me out of deep waters.
PSALM 18:16

Dear Erin,

It seems to me that you don't really know someone until you know their story.

I think it's fair, then, that you know a little bit more about this new relative of yours before I jump in and start sharing with you the essence of what God has put on my heart to convey. And because my story is really the story of *His* work in my life, I hope that you will ultimately come to know more of Him in the process. So here goes.

Like all of us, my journey into adulthood was certainly shaped by my first 18 years of life. But for me, that 18th year was a pivotal one. Not only was it the year I left home for college, but it was also the year that God broke through and got a hold of my heart.

Though I'd grown up in a devoted Christian family that

actively served, I had spent my last few years of high school far from God. I hadn't set out to be that way. But somehow a lack of close, personal discipleship in addition to hanging out with almost all non-Christian friends had gradually led me down a path of wrong choices. As sin took over in my life, I wasn't even plagued by guilt. My conscience had become "seared as with a hot iron," as Paul describes in 1 Timothy 4:2.

God birthed in me not only a renewed walk with Him, but an all-new perspective on life: that it was all about Him.

And yet as it came time to think about college, somehow in the back of my mind I knew that I didn't want to keep going down the road I'd been on. Deep down, I still knew what was right. And so with the strange mix of a wayward heart and yet an inward knowledge of the truth, I set out for school. Looking back, I can see God's hand guiding my steps even though I wasn't seeking Him. I credit His grace all the way.

After arriving on the campus of Wheaton College, one of the first people I met was a vivacious, young sophomore with round-rimmed glasses, a grey backpack and a White Sox hat. Michael caught my eye from day one with his bright smile and spunky personality. Much to my delight, we ended up on a date about a week later. During our long talk that night, however, I learned that Michael's relationship with God was far different from mine. About three years earlier, God had radically transformed him from renegade to Christ follower. I quickly learned that for Michael, life was all about Jesus.

Not only was faith *his* focus, but one couldn't be around him for long without feeling personally challenged as well. As we spent more time together over the course of the next few weeks, I began to realize my hardness to the things of God and the complete folly of my sin. I began to thirst for what Michael had—a vibrant walk with Christ and a devotion to wholeheartedly serve Him with his life.

God birthed in me not only a renewed walk with Him, but an all-new perspective on life: that it was all about Him. And it wasn't just about being saved and going to heaven, but about totally committing to loving and serving Christ.

Wow, was this a 180 degree turn for me! By the time fall break rolled around, my parents hardly recognized who I was because of all the changes taking place inside of me. I certainly didn't mature overnight, but God definitely got a hold of me that fall, for which I'll be forever grateful.

Thankfully changed,
Rachel

- 2 -
the road less traveled

*Enter through the narrow gate. For wide is the gate and broad is the road
that leads to destruction, and many enter through it. But small is the gate
and narrow the road that leads to life, and only a few find it.*
MATTHEW 7:13-14

Dear Erin,

Michael and I got married the summer before our senior
year and absolutely loved being newlyweds. As graduation
neared, we faced the decision of what we would do next. The
world felt wide-open before us. It felt like we could move
practically anywhere and pursue practically anything.

With Michael being a gifted musician, one of our logical
options was to move to Nashville and pursue some kind of
music career. But we also had a heart for ministry. My little
plan was to move to Nashville, pursue the music thing, get
involved in ministry through some local church and that way
we could do both!

I was soon reminded, however, that the man I had married had no desire to pursue anything less than an absolutely

surrendered path towards the will of God for our lives.

Although there was money to be made for talented Christian musicians in a musical hub like Nashville (and maybe even a little fame if I were totally honest with myself), Michael didn't feel drawn to such a venture. In all reality, he felt that to pursue something like that without a clear sense of calling would not be right. With that in mind, we chose to stay where we were and seek God for further direction.

I learned something from that period in our lives.

Jesus taught about the broad and narrow roads. The broad road is, of course, the road most people take—the easy choice, the normal way. But the Bible says that road leads to destruction.

Then there's the narrow road–the road that seems more difficult or perhaps less practical, but beyond its gates lies abundant life (Matthew 7:13-14).

We know that Jesus was talking about the road to eternal destruction versus the road to eternal life. But I believe there's a principle here that also applies to different ways one can live the Christian life.

There is often a "logical" choice, a comfortable road, a path that even Christian friends and family will cheer us down. But it is not always the narrow road. Sometimes it is the broad road infected by:

Worldly thinking
- "This is the responsible thing to do."
- "I want to be successful."

Selfish ambition
- "This will get me what I want."
- "This is my passion, my dream."

Fear
- "The narrow road requires way too much faith and sacrifice."
- "My friends and family would look down on me if I did that."

In the process of making "broad road decisions" we sadly cut ourselves off from what God may have in store for us and how He might use us if we would only take "the road less traveled," to use a term from author M. Scott Peck.

Furthermore, many times Christians go down the broad road not because they feel compelled to do so after soul-searching prayer and surrender, but because the idea simply "makes sense."

Proverbs 21:2 says, "All a man's ways seem right to him, but the Lord weighs the heart."

The journey down the narrow road, on the other hand, is marked by a self-emptied seeking after God's will. It is marked by a surrendered heart wanting to live out His agenda and carry any cross necessary in the process. It is the heart shaped by God. It is the life of the Spirit. And in its wake is a harvest of righteousness–bursting, oozing fruit.

When faced with our potentially life-defining decision years ago, had Michael been the kind of person who just went with the tide—with what looked respectable, but was still really about us and our desires—I believe we may have missed out on many of the incredible joys we have known.

Here's to the narrow road,
Rachel

- 3 -
adventure time

Dear Erin,

As we waited and prayed for direction about what to do now that we had graduated, we received a phone call which God used to steer the course of our lives.

John, who had been a mentor of Michael's since his high school days, called out of the blue one day and wanted to get together. When the two of them met for lunch a few days later, John shared that he and his wife, Cheryl, were praying about going into full-time missions overseas. Would we possibly consider serving with them?

Because we were in the seeking mode, looking for God's direction, and because we were open to serving anywhere, Michael told John, "Sure, we'd consider that!"

Over the next few months, we started meeting regularly with John and Cheryl. Often, we would just get out a world map and ask God to show us where He would have us go. Before long, Michael's newlywed sister and her husband began meeting with us as well. Those foundational times of seeking God together, waiting on Him, and trying to hear what He had to say remain vivid in my mind. And I feel like we are still watching Him answer those prayers all these years later!

Through that whole experience, I learned that earnestly seeking God's will doesn't happen if we aren't looking at life correctly. Evangelist Ron Hutchcraft says that a lot of people come to God with a contract and want Him to sign it, putting His stamp of approval on what they want to do. But God wants people to come to Him with a blank slate. He wants to know if we will sign the bottom of a blank contract before we even know what He is going to write on it. Will we bring ourselves to Him on that level? Will we surrender to Him no matter what He puts down on that paper—be it wealth or want, be it a healthy family or a special needs child, be it Milwaukee or Moscow?

Our lives are to be about His passions and desires, not ours. They are to be about how He wants to bear spiritual fruit for His glory through our unique lives. That's what He created us for! That's where we thrive! And if we believe this, then yielding to all He brings our way and carefully seeking out His voice as we take steps will be paramount in all we do. We'll want to make sure our lives are in line with His heart and His agenda. We'll want to constantly empty ourselves of all that has possibly been conceived of the flesh. We'll want to wipe the slate clean and dare to listen. That's where the adventure of faith begins.

Until next time,
Rachel

- 4 -
into the unknown

Dear Erin,

It is so easy, as Christians, to reject the unknown and stick to the path that is safe and visible before our eyes. I mean, who likes to walk in the dark?

Because of this, many believers spend their whole lives never really getting to know God intimately because they aren't willing to follow Him into the unknown.

But we forget that walking by faith really is walking in the light because *He* is the Light! And He goes with us as we step out into the unknown! He reveals Himself to us in wonderful ways that we could never otherwise know.

The stories of the Israelites provide repeated examples of this walking by faith. (We'll not mention the many times they gave way to fear and lost out!) The picture of faith that stands out most to me is in Joshua 3 when they had to cross the fully swollen Jordan River.

The priests who were to lead the way were instructed by God, "When you reach the edge of the Jordan's waters, go and stand in the river." Often God's leading feels like this. We literally feel like we're being required to step into a river at flood stage.

Yet, we're told that as soon as the priest's feet touched the water's edge, "the water from upstream stopped flowing." Stepping out by faith hadn't left them waist deep in a torrent. It left them standing in the middle of one of the most supernatural wonders of all time!

In our personal story, I've shared how we had been praying regularly with two other couples about how God might lead us to work together in ministry overseas. Well, God didn't necessarily lead how we thought He would. In the end, we had to move forward on faith with as much as He was showing us at the time. We had to step out and trust that He would "part the waters" ahead.

Over the months, John and Cheryl began to sense a leading in one direction while we, through a "Macedonian call" from an African missionary on our answering machine one day, sensed God leading us and our sister and brother-in-law in a different direction. What we thought might end up as a team of six was now a team of two going one way and a team of four going another.

Walking by faith is never boring because we serve a God who rarely reveals the full picture ahead of time

In many ways, we were saddened not to be working with

John and Cheryl. We loved them. But we had sought God and moved ahead according to our best knowledge of His will. We wanted to obey—even if we didn't understand.

Walking by faith is never boring because we serve a God who rarely reveals the full picture ahead of time. He often gives us glimpses into the future, a few pieces of the puzzle at a time, and then reveals more of the details as time goes on.

To walk by faith, we must actively take those steps of waiting on and following God, even if we don't know where we'll end up. Is that not exactly what God called Abraham to do when He said, "Leave your country, your people and your father's household and go to the land I will show you"? Abraham had no idea where God was leading Him, but he had heard the first instruction and was willing to obey it in faith.

The adventures God calls us to are often "risky" from a human standpoint, but "safe" from the standpoint of the One who is able and willing to do great things through those who place themselves fully in His hands. That's when He loves to do what only He can do.

It's my prayer that our lives would be characterized by the deep adventure of faith that can only be taken by listening, trusting and obeying. And if we ever feel little need for faith, we need to ask ourselves if we have slipped into the "safe zone" of walking by sight, where faith is little needed.

With love,
Rachel

- 5 -

through the valley

It was good for me to be afflicted so that I might learn your decrees.
PSALM 119:71

Dear Erin,

And so our sights were set on Africa.

We knew it would likely take at least a year or two before we were actually prepared to move, but we began the necessary training and support-raising to become full-time missionaries.

During this time, I had another desire brewing as well: a desire to be a mom. It was a role I very much looked forward to and I was eager to get started! I brought it up to Michael, who agreed that it seemed like time to start a family. Even though we knew we had a move on the horizon, we trusted that God would work out the timing of it all.

What a relief to no longer have to rope in my desire to be a mother. What joy to stare the reality of children in the face!

That was September and by Christmas, nothing had happened. I was surprised—and disappointed. I felt so "fertile."

But as we sat around the living room with family, I thought, "Surely this will be our last Christmas without kids." It was a delightful thought.

Soon Christmas was over and we settled into winter. My hopes were so high, but would crash each time I realized that this month was not the month. The reality that we were having trouble getting pregnant began to set in. As it did, I remember thinking that this could be deemed as one of the first real trials of my faith. How would I handle it? What would my reaction to suffering be?

I decided right away that I would not get angry with God, for that would be to go against what I knew about His character—that He is good, that He is perfect in all His ways and that He loves me. I resolved not to shake my fist at the only One who could provide comfort as I poured out my heart to Him.

It was about eight months into this period that I began to have trouble seeing pregnant women or women with small children without feeling incredibly heartbroken inside. My maternal desire was enormous but went unfulfilled.

One day a Christian coworker with whom I had shared many of these struggles told me she was pregnant. How I cried. Here, I had been praying for a child for all these months, while she got pregnant right away. As I poured out my heart to God over this, it was as if He spoke tenderly to me, "Rachel, you've asked to be like Jesus. You've asked to be molded into My likeness. I'm doing my work in you."

Doing His work in me? Well, I guess I did want that. I just didn't know it would be so painful. I began to realize a tiny fraction of what Jesus felt when he pleaded for the Father to "take this cup from me" (Mark 14:36).

The cup of suffering is not enjoyable, but God knows that the results bear much fruit. And so He allows it in our lives. And yes, I did begin to see some fruit. With the Psalmist, I could begin to say, "It was good for me to be afflicted so that I might learn your decrees" (Psalm 119:71).

For one thing, some of my pride began to melt away. I soon realized that I controlled neither the timing nor the ability to produce life. All good things were a gift of God, and there was no room for boasting, even if I did get pregnant.

Another fruit of my suffering was that I developed compassion for those in similar circumstances. Sure, I knew infertile couples, but never did my heart go out to them as it did now that I could begin to relate, even in some small way.

As I walked through this trial, I tried to keep in mind three phrases about suffering that I'd read in an article:

God is in control,

God is at work in this situation,

and God knows what's best.

These were not easy truths to hold on to, but I knew that either He was truly good and in control, or it was time to toss in the towel. The first option still felt a lot better and I knew truth was on its side.

In November, Michael and I attended a Christian conference where the speaker talked about "giving God your Isaac." He shared what God has the freedom to do in our lives when we will release to Him those things that are most precious to us.

As I sat there listening (behind a young woman who was eight months pregnant!), I knew God was speaking to me. That afternoon, I went for a walk alone. Standing on a pier overlooking a small lake, I told God that I would surrender to Him my desire to have children. In tears, I told Him that if He never allowed me to be a mother, I would still trust and worship Him.

At that moment, little did I know that our first child had already been conceived.

Of course, that is not everyone's story, but that is how God saw fit to work out this situation in my life. Indeed, there was great gladness of heart when He turned my sorrow into joy.

Remembering like it was yesterday,
Rachel

- 6 -

say what, God?

Although God gives you the bread of adversity and the waters of af-
fliction, your teachers will be hidden no more; with your own eyes you
will see them. Whether you turn to the right or to the left, your ears
will hear a voice behind you saying, "This is the way; walk in it."
ISAIAH 30:20-21

Dear Erin,

Well, by this time, not only was there a baby on the way, but we were headed to Africa. We, along with our wonderful sister and brother-in-law, said many tearful goodbyes at O'Hare International Airport in Chicago before boarding a plane to our new home.

The four of us settled into life in the capital city of Accra, Ghana, with all the ups and downs to be expected in a cross-cultural transition. There was homesickness, getting used to some daily inconveniences and other challenges along the way, but overall we began to feel more comfortable in our new surroundings. Hannah was born six months after our arrival and was a joyful addition to our lives.

Yet after nearly two years of ministry in Ghana, we experienced yet another time where God was shedding less light than we, in our humanness, would have liked. Through various circumstances, specific Scriptures, and the counsel of those we respected, He began to make it clear that our season of ministry in Ghana was coming to an unexpected end.

At the time, it was bewildering. Things made little sense to us. We felt like we were just embarking on what we expected would be years of fruitful service. Things were beginning to roll. Deep relationships had formed. New dreams were evolving. How could we just leave? I was deeply grieved. And what would people think? I felt ashamed.

And yet we felt very strongly that to stay in Ghana would have been to storm past God in defiance. He was making it clear that it was the end of this season. And so, after months of wrestling and praying over the issue, we surrendered. We once again had to take a step of faith without the luxury of sight.

As a young mom of two small children by this point (God surprisingly opened my womb again months after Hannah was born!), I was pretty fragile emotionally over the change. Here I thought we had heard God's call to go to Africa and now, just two years later, we were right back where we had started in Naperville, Illinois. I was no longer a "missionary." I was a normal suburban mom on the outside with a heart inwardly aching over a series of circumstances I didn't understand and African friends I felt we'd abandoned.

But God was faithful. He didn't keep us in the dark forever.

During those months of change, He began to stir within Michael's heart the idea of founding a new ministry based on some of the unique talents, passions and experiences He had given us. When we talked about this with respected mentors in our lives as well as key leaders from the mission organization with whom we had served, we were amazed that each affirmed this new direction. And so, after further prayer and counsel, we began the process of founding OneWay Ministries.

As the months went by, I slowly began to get some glimpses of God's wisdom in all the changes that at first seemed to lack any sense. He also did a deep healing in my heart of the initial pain that I felt.

Years later, I can see in countless ways the profound wisdom of how God led us. I can see how He used the experience of those two years and the relationships that were formed to lay a foundation for the years ahead. In fact, although we are now based in the States, we are more involved in reaching the lost in Ghana through ongoing partnerships than ever before. Hindsight and time have allowed me to see what only faith could "see" then.

I don't know what steps of faith God will set before you. I don't know what He will call you to, how He will lead you or what unexpected circumstances He will send your way in the process of His seeking to gain glory through your life. I just pray that you will have the courage to take the steps of faith He sets before you and find Him amazingly faithful as you do.

On a side note, be aware that walking by faith often has nothing to do with "going" anywhere. Sometimes it just means stepping out and doing something right where you are. Other times it simply means surrendering to the circumstances God has placed into your lap. In offering Him our trust and worship in the midst of hardship, confusion and even grief, God is glorified and His work is put on display through our lives.

Praying you experience this truth as well,
Rachel

35

- 7 -
new beginnings

The boundary lines have fallen for me in pleasant places;
surely I have a delightful inheritance.
PSALM 16:6

Dear Erin,

Well, as we settled down into life in the suburbs, life never got boring as I thought it might. I had mistakenly thought that only by living "on the front lines" in a place like Africa would we experience the excitement of watching God work and the joy of being a part of it. I was proved dead wrong over the years that followed.

As our new ministry was established, I became quite busy with the day to day details of everything from bookkeeping to hospitality. The ministry was operating out of our basement, which brought a steady stream of foot traffic through the front door and a lot of interaction with people coming and going. Relationships also formed with our new neighbors and God began to open up doors for ministry with them as well. So there was a lot going on in addition to having a one and two-year-old to care for. Many days I felt fully spent, but it was a total joy to be a in a place of relying on God and watching Him "do a new thing."

There were more faith-stretching lessons as well. Soon after starting OneWay, we began to plan a short-term mission trip back to Ghana. A small team was formed and we began to meet and pray. A budget was set but, at first, hardly any money came in. Would the team be going after all, I wondered? Had we heard God correctly when we felt this trip was the right thing to do?

And then, as only God can, He amazed us. As the time approached for the team to leave, God provided abundantly for every need from some of the most unlikely sources. Our little organization with almost no track record or regular funding had a team on its way to Ghana for a month-long mission to the unreached peoples of that nation.

By His grace, the team had the privilege of working side by side with many of our former African coworkers, and we saw many come to Christ during those days. One starry night, the team met with a Muslim elder in his nineties who, after hearing the gospel, said that this was the message he'd been waiting for all his life. He received it with joy. Simply amazing.

Yes, it was a season of happiness and healing as we saw God build off of our initial days in Ghana, which once seemed all for naught, and show us that He was not anywhere near done with the good work He had begun. While I could only see life in chapters as I lived it, His eyes could see a much bigger plan.

Grateful to serve a sovereign God,
Rachel

- 8 -
a goliath-sized challenge

This is an easy thing in the eyes of the Lord...
2 KINGS 3:18

Dear Erin,

As the ministry grew, God also blessed us with more children. Ten years after founding OneWay, we had six kids, with our family now occupying almost every corner of our cozy house. The ministry was still operating from our home as well, bursting at the seams in the basement. It was a joyful "fullness," but it seemed clear that something had to give. For OneWay to be able to keep growing, it needed its own place. A little more space to be family was a growing desire as well.

Living in Chicagoland, however, we had no idea how this young ministry could afford a new home that would meet all of its needs. We began to seriously consider relocating to Michigan where costs were much lower. But this would also mean the sad reality of leaving behind some dearly loved coworkers, and many volunteers, friends and supporters as well.

We searched and searched for just the right place in Michigan and came close to thinking we had found it several times, but God never fully opened any of those doors.

I wish I could tell you that I was full of immovable faith throughout this process, but I have to confess that the whole issue started to loom as a "giant in the land" for me. Although I'd read countless stories of God providing for other organizations, I had trouble picturing how He would miraculously make a way for us.

But then I was reminded that the times when we are dealing with "giants" in our lives—those things we can't imagine conquering—are the times when our faith and trust most have an opportunity to shine.

Did I expect to live a "normal" life and experience only "normal" things? Or did I need the courage God admonished Joshua to possess as the Israelites prepared to enter the Promised Land because I, too, was trusting in Him to do the impossible?

God had once again shown the next step when I, in my humanness, could see no solution on the horizon.

Was I relying on Him to do that which, if He didn't do it, wouldn't get done? Was I ready to "stand firm and see the deliverance" He would bring or had I, in my faithlessness, decided that nothing miraculous would come from His hand of might?

I prayed, "Lord, help me to stop deciding when something is 'feasible' or not. Help me to stop leaning on my own understanding. Help me to enter into a whole new sense of trusting You in this area, of believing that You are 'able to do beyond all we could ask or imagine according to Your power that is at work within us' (Ephesians 3:20)."

Although I'm not sure I ever fully conquered my lack of faith, in His perfect timing God did act and in a most amazing way. He moved in the heart of a friend from church to offer our ministry the use of a 7,000-square-foot building his company had just outgrown—rent free until we could afford to pay! It was an absolutely astounding provision in a great location. God had once again shown the next step when I, in my humanness, could see no solution on the horizon.

OneWay's new home was truly more than we ever could have asked for or imagined. It had offices, a large multipurpose room, a beautiful conference room with French doors, a kitchen, ample space for our recording studio, and even room for a much-needed nursery (for part-time staff and volunteers with small children)—all in a prime location just minutes away.

Although we were still in the heart of the suburbs and far from the "front lines" of Africa, we were living a journey of faith, watching God at work in ways we never could have predicted. "The front lines of faith," I was reminded again, exist wherever someone is at the end of their wisdom, abilities and resources and has their eyes fixed on Him.

Hoping you trust Him to conquer your own giants as well,
Rachel

You Are

by Rachel Thompson

We are David, up against the giant
We are Abraham, on the road to the unknown
We are Moses, facing fierce resistance to free people from bondage
We are the young boy, with just a few fish and loaves
We are Gideon's 300, facing an army far greater
We are twelve men, with an assignment to change the world

You are the God who killed Goliath
You are the One who showed Abraham the way
You are the Wonder Worker who freed the people from Egypt
You are the Power that turned a boy's lunch into food for a crowd
You are the Warrior who worked victory for Gideon
You are the Spirit who empowered the Twelve

You are—and that's all that matters

My Story
for personal reflection
or group discussion

1. What are some of the memorable lessons God has taught you about Himself through your own life story?

2. Through the twists and turns of your journey, how have you seen God's faithfulness and how does that encourage you today?

3. If you could write your story going forward, what things would you ask of God in faith?

Recommended Resources

Personal testimonies are one of the most inspiring ways we see God's love, power and sovereignty on display. Read these stories from all over the world and have your faith enlarged!

God's Smuggler by Brother Andrew
An incredible tale of adventure and modern-day miracles, this Dutch brother's story of smuggling Bibles behind the Iron Curtain has amazed and inspired millions of readers for decades.

Outrageous Grace: A Story of Tragedy and Forgiveness by Grace Fabian
Movie producers would have trouble coming up with a more riveting script than this true story delivers. Grace Fabian shares the horrific and yet redemptive account of her missionary husband being murdered in Papua New Guinea while sitting at his desk translating the love chapter, 1 Corinthians 13. Amazing things ensued.

The Hiding Place by Corrie Ten Boom
This famous story is set in Holland during World War II where the Ten Boom family hid Jews from the Nazis. Eventually sent to a concentration camp, Corrie resisted and overcame the evil around her and was eventually released due to a clerical error! An inspiring story, for sure.

The Heavenly Man: The Remarkable True Story of Chinese Christian Brother Yun by Paul Hattaway
Read how God took a poor village boy in China and transformed him into one of China's underground house church leaders. Having suffered much for his faith, Brother Yun has also seen God do the miraculous.

Joni by Joni Eareckson Tada
A dive into a lake at age 16 changed life in an instant for Joni. In this bestselling autobiography, learn how Joni struggled to accept her disability and find meaning in life before ultimately embracing God's loving purposes and finding joy in the midst of suffering.

She Dared to Call Him Father: The Miraculous Story of a Muslim Woman's Encounter with God by Richard H. Schneider
The fascinating story about a prominent Muslim woman who had an unusual and risky conversion to Christ. A compelling story, this book has sold over 300,000 copies.

If I Perish by Esther Ahn Kim
Courageous Kim was condemned to prison after refusing to worship idols in Japan. Read the remarkable account of how she led many to Christ despite the ruthless treatment she endured.

PART 1

The Habits: feeding your soul

He makes me lie down in green pastures,
he leads me beside quiet waters, he restores my soul.
PSALM 23:2-3a

Through some of the key events and life lessons God has used to shape my adult life, I hope you've somehow heard from Him and taken time to reflect on your own journey as well.

As I keep sharing, I want to begin focusing on what I call "The Habits" because they relate to God's overall purpose for our lives and the spiritual disciplines He's given us to keep our relationship with Him at the forefront of it all.

- 9 -

the bedrock decision

I am the vine; you are the branches. If a man remains in me and I in him,
he will bear much fruit; apart from me you can do nothing.
JOHN 15:5

Dear Erin,

In John 15, Jesus described to His disciples the close-knit relationship needed between us, as branches, and Him, the Vine, in order to live an adventure with Him. Connected in this way, we will brim over with fruit as His life fills us and flows out through us.

But how do we have this intimacy? How do we pursue a relationship with the God who made us and become conduits of the fruit He wants us to bear?

Because it's a relationship and not a religion, there is no set formula for knowing God any more than there is for a wife to know her husband. It's a constant back and forth exchange, a shared life, a growing oneness.

And just as a husband and wife nurture their relationship through communication, acts of service, gifts and physical

THE HABITS: FEEDING YOUR SOUL

love, God has given us ways in which we can grow in our intimacy with Him. We often call these things the "spiritual disciplines," those habits and God-given tools by which we draw life from the True Vine and bear the fruit that naturally results.

But note this: just as various married couples have varying degrees of intimacy, so different believers can have varying degrees of closeness with the Lord. Because God never changes, we know that His love for us will be intense, constant, and unconditional. The question is how much we will seek to be near to Him.

In Jeremiah 30:21 God asks, "...who is he who will devote himself to be close to me?" He wants to know who is going to make a lifestyle of striving to be intimate with Him, to know His voice and be His mouth and hands and feet in this world.

In Psalm 81:10 He invites us to fullness and intimacy with these words. "Open wide your mouth and I will fill it." The question we must answer is, "How wide am I opening my mouth?" How much of God do we want? How much are we asking Him to do through our lives?

In James 4:8 we are told, "Come near to God and he will come near to you." Once again, the question is not whether God wants to be close to us. It's a matter of how much we want to be close to Him.

I wish I could say that I maintain a constant intimacy with God and seek Him with unwavering intensity, but I can't. Sometimes I feel dry or distracted, down or defeated. When I've failed at living a disciplined life (again), when I've corrected the kids too harshly (again), or when I've let my prayer life slip into faithlessness and sparseness (again), it can be discouraging.

But I also aim not to accept being in those places, not to accept a lack of joy or victory—at least as far as it depends on my "drawing near." With the psalmist, I have made a bedrock decision to be on a lifelong journey of seeking Him. And it's vital that I regularly ask myself how wholeheartedly I am doing that.

> *Blessed are those whose strength is in you,*
> *who have set their hearts on pilgrimage.*
> *As they pass through the Valley of Baka,*
> *they make it a place of springs;*
> *the autumn rains also cover it with pools.*
> *They go from strength to strength,*
> *till each appears before God in Zion.*
>
> Psalm 84:5-7

With a heart set on pilgrimage,
Rachel

- 10 -
the cornerstone habit

In the morning, O LORD, you hear my voice;
in the morning I lay my requests before you and wait in expectation.
PSALM 5:3

Dear Erin,

As I share thoughts on the foundational habits of living
a godly and fruitful life, I would be remiss not to touch on
what I believe to be the cornerstone habit of seeking God:
regular, unhurried time carved out to be with Him. If there is
one thing we need to get right in order to get everything else
right, this could be it.

The discipline of spending regular time alone with God is
likely nothing new to you. It's often one of the first things we
are taught about living the Christian life. Yet it's something
that even long-time believers sometimes let fall by the way-
side.

I know that none of us is lacking for ways to fill our
days. We all manage to have plenty to do! That's why this
discipline requires us to "carve" time out of our busy days in

order for it to happen.

Jesus had a lot on his plate as well. Whether it was the persistent crowds of people wanting to hear Him speak, the endless lines of sick people needing to get well, or the relational needs of those closest to Him, there were high demands on Jesus' time. And yet we are told in Luke 5:16 that, "Jesus often withdrew to lonely places and prayed."

If Jesus needed that set-apart time to stay connected to the Father, how much more do we!

Imagine that! If Jesus needed that set-apart time to stay connected to the Father, how much more do we! Obviously, Jesus was always communing with God. But there was something about time spent *alone* with His Father, away from everything and everyone else, that sustained Him in a special way.

There are seasons in life when this can be more challenging than others, but honestly, most of us seem to find it hard, no matter what season we're in! I'm afraid the reality is that our hearts tend to run everywhere else first. Eating, exercise, family, friends, work, the phone, the internet, and TV—a lot of us manage to find time for these on a daily basis. But we are very good at making excuses for why we can't find time to be alone with God.

Among the people with the most excuses (and possibly the most valid ones!) are mothers of young children, including yours truly. I have often wondered how in the world I could have struggled to secure regular time with the Lord before we had kids. In fact, I laugh at the thought!

What did I do with all that free time on my hands? But I have found that even with a houseful of young kids at home, when I make it a priority and put forth the effort to get alone with God, He often blesses that time in the most amazing ways, sometimes seeming to even stretch out our time together. In fact, I find myself spending more time alone with Him now than I ever did before becoming a mother. I've realized that time was never the issue. For me, it was always a matter of priority and discipline.

Learning as I go,
Rachel

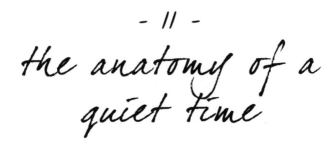

- 11 -
the anatomy of a quiet time

Jesus often withdrew to lonely places and prayed.
LUKE 5:16

Dear Erin,

So we know that Jesus regularly spent time alone with His Father. But what specifics can we learn from this pattern in His life?

First, notice that Jesus "often" withdrew.

Spiritual intimacy cannot be achieved by haphazard and infrequent times with the Savior. We need to be with Him in quiet places frequently. And that takes discipline.

Set a time and a place and make it your regular habit to be there with God. Don't wait until you feel like it. Don't wait until you're not tired. Don't wait until you've gotten all your other work or leisure done for the day. That will simply never happen!

I have discovered, as have many Christian men and

women over the ages, that it's hard to beat meeting with God first thing in the morning. Once your day gets underway, it's hard to stop your mind, quiet your heart, or keep from doing all that needs to be done. It seems Jesus liked this time slot as well.

The key thing is to make time spent alone with God of utmost importance somewhere in your daily life.

Mark 1:35 says, "Very early in the morning, while it was still dark, Jesus got up, left the house and went off to a solitary place, where he prayed."

Now there may be cases where this is not possible or not the best time for your situation. The key thing is to make time spent alone with God of utmost importance somewhere in your daily life.

Second, notice that Jesus withdrew to "lonely" places.

In our day and age, creating a place of solitude may mean silencing your cell phone for a while. It might mean turning off music or other forms of media. It may mean finding a corner of the house where you won't be distracted by others or by visible reminders of things you need to do. (I also like to keep a notebook handy where I can write down any task or thought that pops into my head so I can stay focused and clear-minded.) It might mean taking a walk outside. Whatever the case, it takes determination to "withdraw to lonely places."

Third, notice that when Jesus was alone with His Father, He "prayed."

One of my favorite verses is Psalm 62:8, where we are

encouraged to "pour out" our hearts to God. I just love that He invites us to let Him know everything we're feeling, everything we're facing, and everything we're asking of Him. Just as God the Father already knew everything Jesus was going through, He knows everything that concerns us as well. But He still wants us to come and lay it out before Him. He wants us to release it to Him, to trust Him in it, and listen to what He has to say. Somehow His power is put in motion and we are changed in the process.

Lastly, when you spend time alone with God, I encourage you to learn to linger.

Psalm 25:14 says, "The Lord confides in those who fear Him." There are things on His heart that He wants to share with us. But it takes time and listening. It takes soaking in His Word and letting it fill us. Can you imagine pouring out your heart to someone who kept looking at a watch and seemed itchy to go? I don't think God likes us to deal with Him that way either. If we approach Him like we approach the drive-through at a fast food restaurant, hoping to get a quick bite to eat on our way, He is much less likely to reveal the deep secrets of His heart to us. Our heavenly Father invites us to a sit-down meal where He has prepared for us the richest of foods (Psalm 63:5). Practice lingering at the table.

Bon appétit,
Rachel

- 12 -
abiding through the word

Do not let this Book of the Law depart from your mouth;
meditate on it day and night, so that you may be careful to do
everything written in it. Then you will be prosperous and successful.
JOSHUA 1:8

Dear Erin,

As we linger at God's table and walk with Him throughout a day, Scripture is surely to play one of the most prominent roles in that "abiding" relationship.

Recently, I read a true story about a Russian believer
who had lived through the Communist era, enduring years
of harsh imprisonment in Siberia. For most of that time, he
somehow managed to keep a very tiny copy of the Gospel of
Mark with him, at times seeing it miraculously pass through
meticulous inspections of both his prison cell and his body.

How impacting it was to see just how much that small
book meant to him. It was a true lifeline to his soul, some-

thing he valued more than any other earthly possession. What a great reminder to us of the incalculable worth of the thin-paged Bibles that lie on our night stands.

Although I had grown up with Bibles all of my life, it wasn't until my freshman year of college that the Word of God became a true treasure to me. In the years since, Scripture has played an enormous role in my life and in our experience as a married couple. Without a doubt, it has been a primary tool of God to transform our hearts, shape how we think, and mold our daily walks with Him.

One of the most beautiful things to me about Scripture is how applicable it is. I'm often amazed at how a story I've read tons of times before can suddenly have new meaning as God shows me how it pertains to a current circumstance in my life. How endlessly His Spirit can apply His truths to our hearts!

I also marvel at how God can truly breathe life, strength, comfort and hope into us through His Word. Recently, I was feeling stretched, spent and down. I knew I needed to get alone with God. As I took the first chance that came, I was amazed at how relieving it was to pour out my heart to Him in prayer and then meditate on various Scriptures. I could truly sense Him infusing me with His rest and His strength. An hour later, I felt like a new person simply because of His listening ear, and the comfort and nourishment I had found in meditating on His Word.

Another beautiful thing about Scripture is how it lights our paths (Psalm 119:105). So often, when Michael and I are trying to make decisions about everything from parenting to finances to ministry, God brings to mind a verse, or a series of verses, that steer us in one direction or another. The Holy

Spirit certainly plays a big role in directing us as well, and often He does it directly through the counsel of Scripture.

Another powerful aspect of the Word is how God uses it to cut to our hearts and bring conviction (Acts 2:37). Awhile back I got frustrated with the kids while they were playing in the backyard. Someone was out of line and I spoke too sternly as I corrected him. Moments later, our neighbor stood up from behind the fence. I think she had been crouched down, working on her plants where I couldn't see her. I suddenly thought, "Oh no, did she hear how I was talking to the kids?" Phi-

The more we read His Word and store it up in our hearts, the more it will spill over and impact real life situations.

lippians 4:5 came to mind, "Let your gentleness be evident to all. The Lord is near." I hadn't thought about the Lord being near, much less my neighbor! I'm afraid that my gentleness hadn't been evident and the Spirit convicted me with Scripture.

The list of ways God's Word benefits us could go on and on. It helps us to distinguish between good and evil. It is our sword against the enemy. It trains us in righteousness. It keeps our lives pure. It gives us hope and shows us the way to eternal life (Hebrews 5:14; Ephesians 6:17; 2 Timothy 3:16; Psalm 119:9; 1 John 5:13).

The more we read His Word and store it up in our hearts, the more it will spill over and impact real life situations. I would encourage you, then, to fill your life with the Word of God! Begin your day with Scripture. Pick out a good Bible reading plan and read it. Use a good study guide to dig deeper. Choose some favorite verses and meditate on them. Pick some meaningful verses and memorize them. Post passages on your fridge, your bathroom mirror, and by the kitchen sink. "Write them on the door frames of your houses and on your gates" (Deuteronomy 6:9). Put Scripture up anywhere and everywhere! Listen to an audio Bible when you cook or when you drive or when you fall asleep!

As you let His Word "dwell in you richly," may you be like that beautiful, lush tree "planted by streams of water, which yields its fruit in season" (Colossians 3:16; Psalm 1:3).

Happy Bible reading,
Rachel

- 13 -
the supremacy of wisdom

Wisdom is supreme; therefore get wisdom.
Though it cost all you have, get understanding.
PROVERBS 4:7

Dear Erin,

While it's impossible to elevate one part of the Bible over another, as we talk about foundational things I do want to draw attention to a special book in the Bible that aims to teach us wisdom. Why the free promo? Well, talk about foundational! The Bible says that gaining wisdom is absolutely crucial in life, worth more than all the money we could ever gain. So while we're talking about the Word, wisdom is a subject well worth touching upon.

Years ago I fell in love with the book of Proverbs. From advice on relationships, to handling finances, to being a good wife, the book of Proverbs is one of God's great gifts to us in how to practically live out the Christian life.

Some of the proverbs are easily understood, while others are a bit more obscure. But I have found even the unusual ones to contain rich insights so applicable to life!

A few months ago, I didn't do a good job of managing some of the groceries I had bought and had to throw some things out because they had spoiled. The Holy Spirit brought this proverb to mind as I dumped some things into the garbage, "The lazy man does not roast his game, but the diligent man prizes his possessions" (Proverbs 12:27). I got the point.

When my kids are squabbling and I realize that one of them is instigating things, I apply the proverb, "Drive out the mocker, and out goes strife; quarrels and insults are ended" (Proverbs 22:10) by sending that person to their room. Suddenly peace is restored because the one stirring up the trouble is gone.

There are 31 chapters in Proverbs, with the typical proverbs comprising most of chapters 10-31.

The first nine chapters primarily let us know how important the gaining of wisdom really is. Honestly, I used to find these beginning chapters less than exciting. What I really enjoyed was the down-to-earth, practical advice part of the book! Yet some years back, as I was reading chapters 1-9 again, they stood out to me in a fresh and beautiful way. I began to see them as a megaphone saying, "Hey, everybody! The stuff you are about to read in chapters 10-31 is really important! Pay close attention. Don't reject this advice! The keys to life lie within these pages! Don't be a fool! Lives hang in the balance over these issues! Whatever you do, get wisdom!"

So I would encourage you to give the book of Proverbs—and the seeking of wisdom—a prominent place in your devotional life. Because the book has 31 chapters, some have found that it works well to read a chapter a day, corresponding with the day of the month, in addition to whatever else they are reading in Scripture.

I'd also encourage you to try to memorize proverbs that are particularly meaningful to you. I think you'll find that when you have them on the tip of your tongue, they will more readily come to mind as you face different situations. You will also more naturally be able to share them with others as you give advice on various things.

If you find memory hard, try putting the words to song. Many of the proverbs are so short that it's not too hard to come up with a quick little tune for them. You can even teach them to your kids. Give it a try! Our kids and I have memorized dozens of proverbs this way. If you can't think of a new melody, use a familiar tune and just apply new words.

How about trying to memorize just one new proverb a week? I can guarantee you that with a little effort (and maybe a few memory cards posted around the house) it can be easily done. Most of the proverbs are literally just two short lines long!

The more you internalize this book of Scripture, the more wisdom and understanding you will have to apply to all life circumstances and decisions. So go ahead and soak it in!

With love,
Rachel

- 14 -
abiding through prayer

For everyone who asks receives; he who seeks finds;
and to him who knocks, the door will be opened.
LUKE 11:10

He who is too busy to pray will be too busy to live a holy life.
–E.M. Bounds

Dear Erin,

Plants need several things to grow. Water alone won't do the trick, nor will sunlight or good soil, if not complemented by the others.

In the same way, our spiritual lives cannot thrive on the Word and action alone. There is another dimension—a subtle, yet powerful one—which breathes life into all the rest. Without it, we won't remain in Him. Without it, we won't know the life of the Spirit. Without it, we won't bear much fruit. I'm talking, of course, about prayer.

The Bible has thousands of verses on the matter. Countless books have been devoted to it. With that in mind, I know I can't begin to capture prayer's essence in a few short paragraphs. Plus, I'm still very much a learner myself! All I will attempt to convey, by way of personal testimony, is how prayer gives a depth to our relationship with God that can be gained in no other way. We find in prayer the secret to unlocking God's Spirit in our own lives—and His will on earth.

I remember, as a senior in high school, having almost no understanding of what prayer was. Although I had grown up in a Christian home, prayer was virtually nonexistent in my personal life.

And then, in that first year of college, when God "reached down from on high and took hold of me," my heart was forever changed (Psalm 18:16). A refreshing, new "God-awareness" was born. I could sense His presence. The Bible came alive to me. And for the first time in my life, prayer gave wings to my relationship with God.

Over the years, there have been regular times of me just pouring out my heart to Him (Psalm 62:8). There have been other times of just quietly being together.

There have been times when He begins the conversation, other times when I do. There have been times when He counsels and I listen, times when I ask and He answers–sometimes right on the spot, sometimes years later.

There have been times of deep intercession, of calling out to God on someone's behalf or on behalf of a whole people group or nation. There have been requests for God's intervention in a personal situation. There have been prayers for provision, for guidance, for personal renewal and passion.

Sometimes I've wounded Him, and He's mercifully let me know. As I've confessed, He has forgiven and restored my soul.

There have been times of deep relinquishment and submission and other times of great gratitude and joy.

I have found His voice always gentle, though sometimes firm and piercing. I've found His ears always open, as He often single-handedly comforts some hurting place in me.

The more I've inquired of Him, the firmer my ways have been. The more I've deliberately relied on Him, the more I've seen Him show Himself great in a given situation.

If the Bible has been the foundation of truth in my walk with Christ, surely prayer has been the lifeblood of that relationship. Truly, the two are inseparable. I love these words from John Piper:

> The Word and prayer to me are constantly interwoven. I don't read the Bible longer than a minute without praying, and I don't pray longer than a minute without some Scripture on my mind. If I start churning out prayers that aren't informed pretty explicitly by the Bible, I'm probably going to wind up praying carnal prayers; and if I try to read the Bible extensively without constantly sending my heart up to God, it will become an academic exercise that doesn't move my heart.

I pray that the power of prayer would infuse your walk with Him. May you know, in increasing measure, the beautiful marriage between the Word and prayer, between His truth and His Spirit at work in you!

With love,
Rachel

- 15 -
keeping in step

Since we live by the Spirit, let us keep in step with the Spirit.
GALATIANS 5:25

Dear Erin,

There are times when I wish I could stay in my comfy chair with God all day long. Being alone with Him in those quiet, unhurried moments is truly nourishing to my soul.

But, as you well know, the Christian life involves more than quiet times with God! There are family matters, household tasks, friendships, work and outside ministry involvements—all sorts of things that make up our days. God knows that. He ordained these things and they are all means He uses to bear fruit through us.

When Jesus said, "Abide in me," He wasn't just talking about our devotional lives. He was talking about the whole nine yards! In its essence, abiding in Christ means keeping in step with His Spirit and having His life continually flow out through us. It means keeping a clean slate with God and leaning on Him as we go about our day. It means responding to His nudges. And it means praying continually, having a heart and mind that stays fixed on Him (I Thessalonians 5:17).

One thing I try to do, in addition to having a longer block of time with God in the morning, is to "reconnect" with Him in brief, but deliberate ways throughout the day. It might mean stealing a few minutes in the bathroom away from the kids. It might mean laying down on my bed for five minutes in the afternoon and "touching base" with God after I put the kids down for a nap. It may mean a few minutes of prayerful silence alone in the car or some quiet reading or

When Jesus said, "Abide in me," He wasn't just talking about our devotional lives. He was talking about the whole nine yards.

reflection before bed. Wherever you can, grab a few minutes with Him to refresh and refocus your soul. Lastly, be wary of the electronic devices that can easily fill up these little opportunities with fast bits of information if we allow them to!

Also, be sensitive to the feeling that comes when you may have "slipped out of gear" with God. You know—something's not right, your spirit is upset or anxious, your attitude is sour or hasty, or maybe you've sinned against someone by something you've thought, said or done. Somehow, that sense of "abiding" is gone.

In his wonderful little book, *The Calvary Road*, Roy Hession helps us understand how we can remain in Christ in every moment of the day:

Colossians 3:15 says, 'Let the peace of Christ rule in your hearts.' Everything that disturbs the peace of God in our hearts is sin, no matter how small it is, and no matter how little like sin it may at first appear to be. This peace is to 'rule' our hearts, or (a more literal translation) 'be the referee' in our hearts. When the referee blows his whistle at a football match, the game has to stop, a foul has been committed. When we lose our peace, God's referee in our hearts has blown his whistle! Let us stop immediately, ask God to show us what is wrong, put by faith the sin He shows us under the blood of Jesus, and then peace will be restored and we shall go on our way with our cups running over.

If we are going to be women who bear much fruit, it's crucial that we "keep in step" with God's Spirit. Yes, the foundation for that walk is the time we spend alone with Him. But if it's true that we can do nothing apart from Him, then the abiding better not stop there. We need to stay in tune with Him throughout the day.

Here's to keeping in step as you go,
Rachel

I Only Have to Abide

by Rachel Thompson

Any fruit that comes off of this branch
Comes because of the Vine
His sap, His life flowing through me
I only have to abide

No room for self-exaltation
None of the glory is mine
He does the tending, the pruning, the growing
I only have to abide

And when the crop has failed
When only withered leaves I find
The reason is sure, the remedy clear
I only have to abide

And when the fruit is bursting forth
The Father is glorified
The Son is doing His work in me
I only have to abide

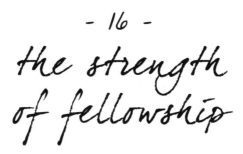

- 16 -
the strength of fellowship

And let us consider how we may spur one another on toward love and good deeds, not giving up meeting together, as some are in the habit of doing, but encouraging one another—and all the more as you see the Day approaching.
HEBREWS 10:24-25

Dear Erin,

We've taken time to look at our spiritual life in its vertical nature—the relationship between us and God. But there is also a critical, horizontal nature to the Christian walk that has to do with us and other believers. We often call it "fellowship," and it is another key habit to build into our lives.

See, God did not intend for the Christian life to be a solo adventure. Right from the start, He said, "It is not good for man to be alone" (Genesis 2:18). He designed us to live in community with others for mutual encouragement, love, and support.

"Two are better than one, because they have a good

return for their labor: If either of them falls down, his friend can help him up. But pity the man who falls and has no one to help him up" (Ecclesiastes 4:9-10).

A spiritual principle is clearly laid out for us here: there is strength in numbers. There is strength in not going at life alone!

Sometimes it's encouragement that we need from others. We need to hear someone tell us that we're doing a good job, that it's worth it to press on, and that we matter. We need to know that we're not the only ones going through such and such. And we need to be reminded that we're loved. Hebrews 3:13 tells us to "encourage one another daily." That's precisely how often we need to hear uplifting words from fellow believers!

Sometimes it's correction that we need. We need someone to lovingly point out a fault or an area where we are off course. We need someone to show us by example a wiser approach to a situation we're facing. We need a friend to remind us to fix our eyes on Jesus instead of the circumstances around us.

We also need training in righteousness. We need people who can teach us how to walk with God more intimately, how to absorb His Word more readily, how to love others more radically. We need face-to-face examples of godly marriages and godly parenting. We need to know others who live out the Scriptures in inspiring and God-honoring ways.

"As iron sharpens iron, so one man sharpens another" (Proverbs 27:17).

Now, this word "sharpen" brings up a good point. See, not all friends sharpen us. Even Christian friends can drag us down if we are not careful or discerning. Just as a metal knife can't be sharpened against a plastic one, so a person who is not wise or walking closely with God is not going to speak into our lives words that challenge, steer and encourage us in the right direction. A few Christian women getting together to gripe about their husbands, for instance, is not godly fellowship! But a friend who will listen, offer biblical counsel and pray for you is. "He who walks with the wise grows wise, but a companion of fools suffers harm" (Proverbs 13:20).

We need to pursue life-on-life engagement. We need to know and be known. We need to "do life together." Without that, it's hard for others to be able to help us grow. They won't even know when we've fallen down, much less be able to help us get up!

I am blessed right now to be a part of a women's group through our church that provides perhaps the richest fellowship I have ever known. Roughly 10-15 of us meet each Sunday before the service for an hour of sharing and prayer. We usually start out with someone sharing a brief Scriptural devotion and then move into a discussion. We often center it around a topic like marriage, parenting, forgiveness, or sharing our faith. Women take turns adding their insights or relevant Scriptures and experiences. Other times we'll just take turns sharing a brief personal update with the group so we know what's going on in each other's lives and hearts. After a person shares, we might spend a few minutes offering encouragement and prayers. Over time, our friendships have grown deep. We represent different ages

Do not settle for a lone-ranger Christian lifestyle!

and backgrounds, but God's Spirit does something powerful when we come together.

So whether it be through your church, a Bible study, Christian friends and/or some other network, I strongly encourage you to pursue meaningful, godly fellowship. Do not settle for a lone-ranger Christian lifestyle!

Pray for godly friends and mentors with whom you can walk through life. Ask God to provide people who will spur you on and cause you to grow. If your spouse or children fill up some of this need, thank Him. If they don't, ask Him to fully meet the need in other ways. Tell Him that you long for the joy and lightening of the load that fellowship brings.

It's also worth noting that although personal relationships are the primary means of Christian fellowship, it is also possible to receive encouragement, correction and training from fellow believers through the written word. Sometimes a good book full of spiritual wisdom can be just what the doctor ordered. Hannah Whitall Smith died years ago, but her devotional classic, *The Christian's Secret of a Happy Life*, for instance, might readily uplift or counsel you through a hard season. Or the blog by that wise Christian woman who's been where you are may be just the encouragement you need for today.

Lastly, as you seek out fellowship, also remember to focus on providing it for others. Who are *you* encouraging? Who can *you* call and invite over for coffee? Who could benefit from the strength of *your* friendship? Yes, look to be upheld. But don't forget that someone else needs your upholding, too!

In its essence, that's what Christian fellowship is all about.

Here's to walking together,
Rachel

The Habits
for personal reflection
or group discussion

1. Do you regularly have meaningful time in God's Word? If so, how do you notice it impacting your life?

2. How would you describe your prayer life? How do you think it could grow?

3. Do you find it difficult to "keep in step" with God through a day? What things do you find helpful in order to practice this discipline?

4. What are your main sources of Christian fellowship? How are you being built up and how are you building others up?

Recommended Resources

A Place of Quiet Rest: Finding Intimacy with God Through a Daily Devotional Life by Nancy Leigh DeMoss
Encouragement–and tools–to seek God for a lifetime.

Spiritual Disciplines for the Christian Life by Donald S. Whitney
Readable and applicable, the author touches on 12 key disciplines for spiritual growth.

How to Study the Bible for Yourself by Tim LaHaye
An excellent resource to help you gain understanding and get the most out of your time in God's Word.

Lord, Teach Me to Pray in 28 Days by Kay Arthur
Through practical insights drawn from the Lord's Prayer, learn "how to pray, what to pray, and what to expect" when you pray.

Let Us Pray by Watchman Nee
Against a backdrop of Scriptural insights, learn how to pray from this classic Chinese Christian author who endured much suffering for Christ.

The True Vine by Andrew Murray
In this 31-day devotional classic based on John 15, learn what it really means to have an abiding relationship with Christ.

www.forevergratefulmusic.com and *www.seedsfamilyworship.net*
Two great resources for hiding God's Word in your heart through wonderful Scripture memory songs. Well-written and well-recorded, these albums make memorizing God's Word a breeze!

PART II

The Heart: reflecting your God

And we, who with unveiled faces all reflect the Lord's glory,
are being transformed into His likeness with ever-increasing glory...
2 CORINTHIANS 3:18

We've spent time looking at some of the key disciplines of a godly woman—disciplines by which God feeds our souls and shapes our hearts. But how exactly is He trying to shape us? What character traits does He want to see formed in us so that we increasingly reflect Him and become the fragrance of Christ wherever we go?

There is, of course, the well-known list of characteristics the Holy Spirit produces in us when we are walking in Him: love, joy, peace, patience, kindness, goodness, gentleness, faithfulness and self-control (Galatians 5:22). There are also those mentioned in 2 Peter 1: faith, goodness, knowledge, self-control, perseverance, godliness, brotherly kindness and love. From other Scriptures we could add even more traits to our growing list.

To write about each of these at length could take years! In the following letters, I simply want to touch on a handful of qualities that have been especially significant to me in the quest to be a woman whose heart looks more and more like His.

- *17* -

nobility: rare and deep stuff

A wife of noble character who can find?
She is worth far more than rubies.
PROVERBS 31:10

Dear Erin,

Attractive women are not hard to find. But women with
deeply respectable characters are a rare and priceless jewel.

Chuck Swindoll points out that women can change their
external appearance drastically in quite a short time. Roll
out of bed looking unkempt and within half an hour, things
can be greatly improved! But developing inner beauty, he
stresses, is a lifelong endeavor.

I think one of the reasons why women of noble character are so hard to find is due to the simple fact that relatively
few women focus great amounts of energy on developing
this inner beauty.

Have you ever had the privilege of knowing a woman who stood out to you in wisdom, in temperance, or in speech? Have you ever encountered someone you wanted to be around just so that maybe some of who she was would rub off on you? When uncommon, godly character has been forged in a woman's life, it is an extremely beautiful thing.

I love the biblical story of Ruth. Here was a woman who had lost her husband and could have gone back to her own family and country. Instead, she chose to move to a new city with her widowed mother-in-law, Naomi. As they settled down, Ruth worked long, hard hours in order to put food on the table for the two of them. She didn't spend her energies

When uncommon, godly character has been forged in a woman's life, it is an extremely beautiful thing.

on outward appearance or attracting another husband, but rather showed extreme loyalty and love to this woman who wasn't even a blood relative.

Ruth's noble character was radiant and others took notice. In the end, she was blessed with a husband, Boaz, one of the most respected and God-fearing men in town. He was drawn to her not because of her appearance, but because of who she was on the inside. "All my fellow townsmen know that you are a woman of noble character," he told her.

If we have hearts like Ruth, hearts that love God and sacrificially serve others, if we are more concerned about our character than our appearance, we will be blessed. The lasting fruit borne out of our lives will reap man's greatest compliments and heaven's highest praise.

"Her children arise and call her blessed; her husband also and he praises her: 'Many women do noble things, but you surpass them all'...Give her the reward she has earned, and let her works bring her praise at the city gate" (Proverbs 31: 28-29, 31).

May you live a life of such noble character that those around you can't help but notice that there is so much more to who you are on the inside than what they see on the outside.

For a heart like Ruth's,
Rachel

- 18 -
quietness and gentleness: a great duo

Your beauty should not come from outward adornment...
Instead, it should be that of your inner self, the unfading beauty of a
gentle and quiet spirit, which is of great worth in God's sight.
1 PETER 3:3-4

Dear Erin,

Ahhh. A gentle and quiet spirit. Those words alone are enough to soothe me!

But it can be hard for us to be quiet. For some reason, we often gravitate towards noise and activity, news and information. We gravitate toward talking.

Of course words, in and of themselves, are not bad. In fact, Scripture describes all sorts of ways that words can be a "fountain of life" to those who hear them. With our tongues we can praise God, encourage our husbands, nurture our kids, or share Christ with a friend.

The problem is that often our tongues don't have those good functions. Our words would often better be replaced with silence when they fall under the categories of gossip, slander, idle chatter, complaining, nagging, arguing, or criticizing. And even if we don't mean that to be the case, the more we talk, the more likely it is that something will spill out that is less than edifying. "When words are many sin is not absent, but he who holds his tongue is wise" (Proverbs 10:19).

Having a quiet spirit doesn't mean never speaking up. But it does mean weighing our words rather than letting them gush out (Proverbs 15:28). It means asking God for the right word for the moment. It means reflecting often and retreating regularly. It means being okay to be still and silent before the Lord.

The quiet heart doesn't have to be in the spotlight, and it doesn't have to be in charge. It doesn't always have to be heard. The quiet heart doesn't feed on the praise of men. At its deepest level, it is fed by the Lord Himself.

The quiet heart doesn't feed on the praise of men. At its deepest level, it is fed by the Lord Himself.

All in all, there is something about the quiet heart that is extremely refreshing and God-like.

And then there's gentleness—another wonderful attribute that immediately speaks to inner beauty. Gentleness is not especially hard to come by when everything is going well. It's when there's friction or hurry or chaos that we tend to resort to harsher tones and actions.

Sometimes when I hear the way I talk to my kids, I think to myself, "Now why couldn't you have just said the same thing, but said it gently? Why did it have to have an edge?" Oh, that we would constantly wear the garments of gentleness in our interactions with others. What a wonderful testimony to our gentle Savior!

Like all godly traits, quietness and gentleness are hard fruits to tack on from the outside. They are born out of the inner life, a close walk with Christ, and a heart that is "quick to listen, slow to speak and slow to become angry" (James 1:19). And when these two traits are cultivated side by side, my goodness, what a beautiful pair!

Many a husband and child have wished the woman in their lives possessed the priceless virtues of gentleness and quietness. Many times I have wished I possessed them in greater measure myself.

Still growing,
Rachel

- 19 -
strength and dignity: steady eddy

She is clothed with strength and dignity;
she can laugh at the days to come.
PROVERBS 31:25

Dear Erin,

You likely know someone whose moods waver greatly from day to day. You never know if they are going to be chipper and cheerful or gloomy and glum.

The woman who abides deeply in Christ displays an inner strength that is not easily ruffled by circumstances or emotions. There is a steadiness of spirit about her, a sense of dignity, a calm composure. Her husband and kids don't have to guess what kind of mood she will be in on a given day. Her friends can count on her stability.

Whether it be a tough relational moment, sudden and unexpected bad news, or just a mountain of emotions that well up inside of you for whatever reason, seek to be a woman marked by strength and dignity.

This doesn't mean you never cry or feel disappointed, deflated or crushed. It doesn't mean you never pour out your heart to God in tears. It doesn't mean you never look "weak" to those around you. But it does mean that there is a deep confidence that sustains you and shapes how you react to life's pressures and curve balls. There is an enduring hope that allows you to "give thanks in all circumstances" (I Thessalonians 5:18).

While none of us likes to go through tough days, pain or hardship, difficult circumstances definitely reveal our character. Proverbs 24:10 says, "If you falter in times of trouble, how small is your strength!"

A woman of strength and dignity has an abiding knowledge of God's comfort that keeps her running to Him as her refuge and strength.

A woman of strength and dignity has an abiding knowledge of God's comfort that keeps her running to Him as her "refuge and strength, an ever-present help in trouble" (Psalm 46:1).

My Aunt Lois was an amazing example to me of a woman who didn't falter under pressure. Her world turned upside down one day when her 47-year old husband was fatally wounded in a motorcycle accident while they were serving as missionaries in West Africa. As he clung to life in the hospital, she prayed, "God, Ellsworth was Yours long before he was mine. It's not my desire for You to take him, but if that is Your will, then I give him back to You." And then she added, "These are very expensive lessons. Don't let us waste them."

That kind of character can't be manufactured in the heat of the moment. And it certainly can't be fabricated when life strips us of the things we hold most dear. These godly qualities can only be forged by a deep and abiding walk with Christ, and an incessant clinging to the immovable Rock.

So don't let anything rob you of the inner calmness that is yours when you keep in step with God's Spirit. Don't let your dignity vanish in a moment of anger. Don't let your strength crumble when heartache looms. Rather, make these beautiful words from Psalm 73 the prayer and cry of your soul. "My heart and my flesh may fail, but God is the strength of my heart and my portion forever."

Steady on,
Rachel

- 20 -
kindness:
simple but powerful

A kindhearted woman gains respect,
but ruthless men gain only wealth.
PROVERBS 11:16

Dear Erin,

Friendly, warm-hearted, understanding, generous, considerate, agreeable. Don't you just love being around people like that?

Well, believe it or not, all those words come from the dictionary definition of a very simple, but powerful word. It's a word that the apostle Paul specifically said is to characterize young women in the church. It's a word that is so simple, I hope you won't laugh when you read it. We are to be kind (Titus 2:5).

Kindness is love in action. It is considering the needs of others above your own and thoughtfully seeking to meet them. It's being gracious in speech and pleasant when giving instruction (Proverbs 16:21). It's being so warm-hearted and understanding that everyone from small children to broken adults seek out your listening ear. When I think about kindness in these terms, I have a better understanding of why Paul thought it was such a crucial trait for a young woman who wants to flourish in Christ.

So what does it look like when someone lacks this life-giving fruit of the Spirit?

One word that comes to mind is "abrasive." Abrasive people are easily offended. They are hard to please. They easily find fault. They hold grudges. They lack a forgiving spirit. They thrive on conflict. They repel people rather than nurture them. Simply put, they lack a spirit of kindness (Proverbs 11:27; Ephesians 4:32).

Another word that comes to mind is "self-absorbed." In order to be kind, one has to be focused on others. One has to be compelled by the love of God to meet the needs of those in her family and outside her home. The woman who gets wrapped up in her own little world becomes blind or complacent to the needs of others.

The woman truly marked by kindness gains the respect of those she loves and the praise of her Father in heaven (Proverbs 11:16; Proverbs 31:31).

A few years ago, I remember wishing that my 5-year-old son showed me more respect. I would try to exact it of him. I could get the outward action I wanted, but his heart didn't seem to follow. I was frustrated.

Then God began to reveal to me that I wasn't dealing with him in kindness. In fact, I was often harsh and demanding. My son's spirit was being crushed, leaving him to feel little respect for me in his heart.

After being convicted of my sin, my way of dealing with our precious son began to change. I had more compassion on him. My words became more pleasant. I made it a point to encourage him more. I expressed delight in him. I played with him more. And over time, I saw him change. The boy who would never willingly let me hug him or kiss him on the cheek was now open to affection. When I'd say, "Good night, I love you" at bedtime, he would answer back that he loved me too.

An iron fist hadn't opened his heart. What finally brought our relationship to a new level was plain and simple kindness. "Pleasant words promote instruction" and "a kindhearted woman gains respect" (Proverbs 16:21; Proverbs 11:16). What golden phrases to capture the heart of kindness for us!

And it seemed like such a little word.

With love,
Rachel

- 21 -

trust:
oh for more of it!

Who among you fears the LORD and obeys the word of his servant?
Let him who walks in the dark, who has no light, trust in the name of
the LORD and rely on his God.
ISAIAH 50:10

Dear Erin,

I love the line in the hymn "'Tis So Sweet to Trust in Jesus" that says, "Oh, for grace to trust Him more." If there is one character quality I long to truly possess more of, it is trust. So many things in life tempt us not to trust God, but how contrary this is to the essence of faith.

Trust is a decision we make regarding things we are not sure of because of things we are convinced of: that God, who does not change, is perfect and loving in all of His ways (Hebrews 13:8; Psalm 145:17).

I've realized that one reason it can be hard to say, "I trust you, Lord" is because in doing so I must give up my security blankets of doubt and fear. I mean, if I really trust God, then

I have to let go of the things that are in opposition to that trust, right?

This doesn't mean, by the way, that I am not free to grieve when a loss or sadness occurs. God bears our burdens and feels our grief. But we must resist the sinful tendencies that take us beyond grief to doubt and fear.

Is there anything God could allow to happen in your life that would change your view of Him? Until we get to the point where we can say with Job, "Though He slay me, yet I will hope in Him," our trust is at the disposal of circumstances as much as an ocean wave is to the wind.

Trusting Him when we can see how everything is going to work out is not true trust. Trust is placing our confidence in Him and believing His promises when we have no idea how the pain will ever be less, no idea how He can work this out for His glory, and no idea how He is possibly still in control.

In her classic devotional, *Streams in the Desert*, L. B. Cowman shares:

> The way to peace and victory is to accept every circumstance and every trial as being straight from the hand of our loving Father; to live "with Him in the heavenly realms" (Ephesians 2:6), above the clouds, in the very presence of His throne; and to look down from glory on our circumstances as being lovingly, divinely appointed.

Most of us struggle to live "above the clouds," however, when experiencing what author Catherine Marshall calls "the dark night of the soul." These are those times when we are completely crushed or bewildered, where nothing seems to make sense and no light seems to shine on our circumstances or our inner being. God seems distant, while fear, doubt and depression creep in.

One of Marshall's "dark nights of the soul" came when her infant granddaughter struggled for life, only to lose the battle. Catherine had prayed so hard. She was devastated. "What's destroying me is that I don't understand," she wrote. "I, from my tiny human vantage point, am demanding to see into the secrets of eternity."

Her friend challenged her on it, leading to a whole new realization. In *Light in My Darkest Night* Marshall relates:

> When Amy Catherine died, I demanded that God explain Himself to me, and when He didn't, I proceeded to sulk like a child who had failed to get her own way... Then came this revelation. When life hands us situations we cannot understand, we have one of two choices. We can wallow in misery, separated from God. Or we can tell Him, "I need You and Your presence in my life more than I need understanding. I choose You, Lord. I trust You to give me understanding and an answer to all of my why's only if and when You choose."

Isn't it true that what often angers or frustrates us about God are the things we do not understand?

I remember when singer Steven Curtis Chapman lost his precious 5-year-old adopted daughter in a gut-wrenching accident in their driveway. It seemed so senseless. I was upset and realized a few weeks later that in my heart I had been "charging God with wrongdoing" (Job 1:22).

Yet just because I couldn't make sense of it, just because I couldn't see the bigger picture, had God's character changed from good to bad? Had He gone from perfect to imperfect? Were His ways and thoughts no longer higher than mine (Isaiah 55:9)? In reality, I was foolishly assuming that I somehow knew better than He did what was best.

Catherine Marshall summed up the lesson she learned this way:

> Understanding. That seems to be the key word in my difficulties. I have sought it from the Lord most of my life and in His gentle tenderness He has often provided it. So often, in fact, that I had begun to take it for granted, assumed I had a right to understanding. What arrogance! What presumption!

May we never seek or demand understanding more than we simply seek the One whose perfect understanding no one can fathom (Isaiah 40:28).

> *My heart is not proud, O Lord,*
> *my eyes are not haughty;*
> *I do not concern myself with great matters*
> *or things too wonderful for me.*
> *But I have stilled and quieted my soul;*
> *like a weaned child with its mother,*
> *like a weaned child is my soul within me.*
> *O Israel, put your hope in the Lord*
> *both now and forevermore.*
>
> Psalm 131

Hoping in Him and learning to trust,
Rachel

- 22 -
self-control: standing strong

*Like a city whose walls are broken down
is a man who lacks self-control.*
PROVERBS 25:28

Dear Erin,

The images of Hurricane Katrina hitting New Orleans in 2005 will stay with us for a long time. It's hard to forget the footage of the levies meant to defend the city against the sea, collapsing under the pressure of the surging waters. The devastation was horrific.

Among the many lessons from that storm is a clear message about the danger of lacking self-control. Whole lives can be ruined for lack of this virtue!

When we lack self-control, we are totally vulnerable. Like a city with broken down walls, we have lost our defenses. We are vulnerable to attack from the enemy, vulnerable to impurities, and vulnerable to things that can replace Christ as our Master.

We have an enemy who is looking for breaches in our walls. First Peter 5:8 says, "Be self-controlled and alert. Your enemy the devil prowls around like a roaring lion looking for someone to devour." When he finds a heart or mind with vulnerable walls, there is nothing he likes more than to go in for the kill.

Years back, I experienced the ruthless tactics of the enemy in attempting to create a crack in our marriage. Thoughts about a male friend of ours kept popping to mind. At first I was naïve. "He's a really nice person," I would think to myself. "I'm sure glad we know him." Then I realized that Satan was bombarding me with thoughts beyond that, and I was not doing a good job of repelling them.

About that time I was also reading the story of Joseph. What did he do when Potiphar's wife tried to seduce him? He took off running!!! He made a point to go in the exact opposite direction of the temptation and to do so in a forceful hurry. I realized that that was how I needed to handle the fiery darts the enemy was throwing my way.

It was an exercise in mental self-control as I aimed to consciously "take captive every thought to make it obedient to Christ" (2 Corinthians 10:5). The darts soon became nullified by a strong wall of defense. Before long, they seemed to stop flying at all. "Submit yourselves, then, to God. Resist the devil, and he will flee from you" (James 4:7).

As married women, we don't just need self-control over our thought life. We also need it in the area of our emotions. Lack of self-control, for instance, can leave us subject to outbursts of anger, self-pity, or pouting.

I remember trying to use the "pouting tactic" on Michael early on in our dating relationship when he had said something that hurt me. I tried to punish him with silence. Thankfully, he didn't stand for it. He called me on my game. He gently, but firmly, let me know that this was no way to deal with each other, and that we would not operate like that in our relationship. It was a tough pill to swallow, but it started to change the way I dealt with my emotions.

I now realize that my pouting was a sinful choice (as much as I would like to think it was the only possible re-action when offended). Through the Spirit's enabling, I've realized that I am just as able to choose overlooking the offense (Proverbs 19:11), openly talking about it or taking to heart a correction I needed to hear. Self-control means that I am not a slave to my emotions. I can choose an upright way of acting on them.

Lack of self-control can also leave us subject to the desires of the flesh in the areas of food, sleep, shopping, entertainment choices or any number of things we might crave.

When we lack self-control, we are totally vulnerable. Like a city with broken down walls, we have lost our defenses.

I have long struggled with a love for desserts. But a while back I was convicted by the words in 2 Peter 2:19 that say, "a man is a slave to whatever has mastered him." I certainly didn't want a big hunk of brownies to be lord over me. That's pretty low!

So, when reaching for a dessert, I try to ask myself, "Are you a slave or the master at this moment?" If I sense that I am not in complete control or in full step with the Spirit, I know

THE HEART: REFLECTING YOUR GOD

what I need to do.

When I don't feel like getting out of bed early to meet with the Lord, sometimes I think of Paul when he said, "I beat my body and make it my slave" (1Corinthians 9:27). He knew what it was to overpower the flesh through the Spirit, who gives self-control.

So rely on God's Word and His Spirit to keep your wall strong. So much depends on it.

Resolutely,
Rachel

- 23 -
modesty:
celebrating hiddenness

Like a gold ring in a pig's snout
is a beautiful woman who shows no discretion.
PROVERBS 11:22

Dear Erin,

If you can imagine a hog wearing jewelry, then you can imagine just how unsightly it would be. The jewelry would be totally out of place, its beauty grossly marred by the inappropriate presentation. What an unlikely comparison King Solomon made when he compared this picture to immodesty, yet there is so much truth packed into this proverb.

When God created humans, he didn't make us square boxes with no form or beauty. He formed each of us with His hands and made us in His image. We are beautiful creatures even as He is a beautiful God.

But godly beauty is always meant to be in the context of purity. That's when it's truly beautiful. When godly beauty

100

gets marred by human sin, the result is less than lovely. In fact, like a gold ring against the backdrop of a pig, it can be downright disgusting!

It saddens me when I see young Christian women marring their God-given beauty by dressing inappropriately. Clothes that leave little to the imagination or that flaunt certain body features have no place in the life of a woman striving for godliness. Inappropriate clothes have a way of boasting, tempting, and distracting. They call attention to the flesh instead of the spirit. They encourage lustful thoughts in the minds of our brothers in Christ and so easily become a hindrance to those trying to keep their thoughts pure.

Yes, God created us with the ability to be attracted to the opposite sex. It's a wonderful thing! But He wants that attractiveness to bloom within the right context. Song of Solomon 8:4 says, "Do not arouse or awaken love until it so desires." There is a time and a place for attraction and love to grow. Lack of modesty can cause attraction to bloom in the wrong place with the wrong person at the wrong time.

Sometimes we dress immodestly simply because we have let the culture around us dictate what's appropriate. We've allowed the world to "squeeze us into its mold," as The Living Bible puts it in Romans 12:2. We might wear things that are too low, too high, or just too revealing of what's underneath—all without realizing we are being immodest.

Also, because our culture has gotten so far away from godly ideals, deciding what's modest by comparing our styles with things that are *really* immodest is errant thinking. For example, many T-shirts that our society would consider modest are actually quite immodest simply because they "hug" the body too tightly. Or just because some people wear shorts that don't cover much more than their underwear, it may be easy to think that covering a few more inches is surely adequate.

Several times I have found great deals at my favorite thrift store on a pair of jeans or a skirt. I've worn them once or twice and then felt the conviction of the Holy Spirit that the item was a potential stumbling block because it either fit too snuggly or just drew too much attention visually. And I've sadly, but confidently, gotten rid of them.

Godly beauty is always meant to be in the context of purity. That's when it's truly beautiful.

Another issue in dressing modestly has less to do with being sexy and more to do with style or expense. Some women spend an enormous amount of time and money on clothing, hair, jewelry and shoes—and it shows. It can create walls of intimidation in relationships. And it definitely tends to direct attention away from the spiritual to the physical. This type of excess can emit an odor of vanity. Is that really what we want?

I encourage you to make your wardrobe an area of prayer. Bring the issue before God and ask Him to show you if there's anything in your motives that is impure, or if anything in your closet is not fitting for you to wear. Ask a godly woman whom you respect what she thinks of the way you dress.

In our quest to be godly women, don't we want the freedom of walking around knowing that we have done our best not to be a stumbling block for men or a point of envy for other women? The apostle Paul admonishes us to "dress modestly" and to clothe ourselves "with good deeds, appropriate for women who profess to worship God" (1 Timothy 2:9-10).

Of course this doesn't mean we should wear cloth flour sacs and look entirely unfeminine or unattractive as long as we are beautiful on the inside! No, just like we wouldn't like it if our husbands never combed their hair or brushed their teeth, we should aim to present ourselves well. It's just that there are biblical principles we need to keep in mind as we do so.

As John Piper beautifully put it:

> Clothes are not meant to make people think about what is under the clothes. Clothes are meant to direct attention to what is not under them: merciful hands that serve others in the name of Christ, beautiful feet that carry the gospel where it is needed, and the brightness of a face that has beheld the glory of Jesus.

I think that sums it up pretty well. Don't you?

With love,
Rachel

* For a brief, practical resource on this issue, check out *The Look: Does God Really Care What I Wear?* by Nancy Leigh DeMoss.

- 24 -
thankfulness: more than just a november thing

Dear Erin,

Are you someone who frequently sends up little verbal thank you notes to God for all His blessings? I have found cultivating a heart of gratitude to be a life-giving, attitude-defining practice.

In Luke 17, we read the brief account of Jesus healing ten men with leprosy. Only one of them came back to say thank you, at which point Jesus asked him, "Where are the other nine?" Just as we appreciate being thanked for things, we learn here that God does too.

Learn to appreciate His blessings—your breakfast, your health, morning sunshine, your toddler sleeping in longer than usual, or (maybe this one is just for me) finding just what you needed at your neighborhood garage sale! If "every good and perfect gift comes from above" (James 1:17), then don't be afraid to give God credit for His good gifts throughout a day.

Remember to thank Him for His bigger gifts as well. When was the last time you

"Be joyful always, pray continually, give thanks in all circumstances" **(1 Thes. 5:16-18)**

poured out thanks for the grace He has shown you in your salvation? When was the last time you privately praised God for His forgiveness, from the bottom of your heart?

Thank Him for your trials, too. Really? Really. First Thessalonians 5:18 says we should, "Give thanks in all circumstances, for this is God's will for you in Christ Jesus." James 1:2 boldly tells us to, "Consider it pure joy" whenever we face trials of many kinds. Pure joy? Wow.

It's definitely far from our natural reaction to thank God when things go wrong, but there is power in obedience when we praise Him in the midst of our difficulties. He's still in control. He still loves us. And for those who love Him, He is at work for our good and His purposes (Romans 8:28). So go ahead. Force yourself to utter thanks for His goodness and love in the midst of what you are going through and for His sovereign hand over it.

I have learned so much about having a grateful, rejoicing

spirit from an amazing woman aptly named Joy Ridderhoff. Founder of Global Recordings Network (GRN), she pioneered the audio recording of the gospel message in hundreds upon hundreds of languages beginning in the 1930's. The GRN library now has the gospel message available in audio format in more than 6,000 languages. Countless unreached people who cannot read have heard the story of Jesus because of the ministry she started. But mind you, her work was not always easy.

As she would travel and record in the most remote of places, she often battled travel difficulties, recording equipment that quit working, financial shortages, and bad weather that prevented scheduled recordings from taking place. Yet no matter what happened, she resolved to give thanks and rejoice. Time and again, not only were her spirits lifted, but she saw God pour out His blessing in incredible ways as a result of her simple act of obedience. The crystal clear theme of her life was to "rejoice always" (Philippians 4:4).*

In her wake, I have tried to literally apply that biblical principle and have seen how it changes things. One night I was going to bed feeling sorry for myself about something and my flesh wanted to indulge in pouting. But the Holy Spirit brought to mind these words, "Be joyful always, pray continually, give thanks in all circumstances" (1 Thessalonians 5:16-18). And so I obeyed. Almost immediately, my mood changed.

Whether or not we see God's relief or blessing right away, there is great virtue and reward in overflowing with thanks as an act of obedience.

If we don't generally overflow with thanks, perhaps we've lost perspective and are failing to notice God's goodness in our lives. Or maybe we've unknowingly come to think we somehow deserve His grace and His gifts. Remember how Jonah got mad at God for taking away the plant that had provided him shade? Even though the plant was a gift, Jonah had come to think He had a right to it (Jonah 4:9). Amazingly, we often fall into the same trap!

So let's determine to give thanks for every good gift that comes from above, and for every trial that tests our faith. Throughout our days, let's be people who truly spill over with gratitude.

Because He's worthy of it,
Rachel

*GRN has compiled some of Joy Ridderhoff's writings into a powerful little devotional called *Rejoice Always*. Call 888-444-7872 in the U.S. to order a copy. It is a life-changing book!

- 25 -
forgiveness: freely you have received

Bear with each other and forgive whatever grievances you may have
against one another. Forgive as the Lord forgave you.
COLOSSIANS 3:13

Dear Erin,

One the most profound statements I've ever heard on the issue of forgiveness came from a good African friend of ours. I was struggling with someone whom I needed to forgive and I asked our friend how he forgave people who had wronged him. He replied easily, "Oh, I just forgive people ahead of time. I know they'll wrong me at some point, so I just forgive them first!"

Now those are the words of a man who understands what it means to receive God's mercy and pass it on.

In Matthew 18, Jesus tells the story of a servant who owed his master ten thousand talents. Because he couldn't repay the money, he and his whole family were to be sold to satisfy the debt. But the servant fell on his knees and begged his master to reconsider. The master had pity on him and the debt was cancelled.

A few verses later, we find the servant going off and nearly choking a man who owed him a mere fraction of the debt the servant had been forgiven. Though the man begged for mercy, he was thrown into prison.

Needless to say, the master wasn't happy. "'You wicked servant,' he said, 'I canceled all that debt of yours because you begged me to. Shouldn't you have had mercy on your fellow servant just as I had on you?' In anger, his master turned him over to the jailers to be tortured until he should pay back all that he owed" (Matthew 18:32-34).

After telling the story, Jesus finished with this statement. "This is how my heavenly Father will treat each of you unless you forgive your brother from your heart."

How convicting! Jesus is telling us that we will have to bear our own sin debt before Him if we refuse to forgive others their sin debts against us. And we're not just told to forgive, we're told to do it from our hearts.

See, as believers in Christ we have been forgiven an enormous debt that we could never begin to repay. Yet we are inclined to hold things against those who wrong us, to not genuinely forgive them. We habitually foster grudges and harbor bitterness for the wrongs we've incurred.

Such behavior is foolishness and it arouses God's anger. It reveals that we often lose sight of the mercy we have received.

Remember, we don't forgive others by the measure they deserve. Rather, we forgive them according to the measure we have received from God. Have I been forgiven much?

Yes. Do I often repeat the same old sins and come begging for God's forgiveness once again? Yes. Does He have a limit on how much or how often He will forgive me? No. Then I must forgive in the same way.

If we refuse to forgive others, we're told that God will also refuse to forgive us. "But if you do not forgive men their sins, your Father will not forgive your sins" (Matthew 6:15). Jesus also said, "And when you stand praying, if you hold anything against anyone, forgive him, so that your Father in heaven may forgive you your sins" (Mark 11:25).

It's also important to note the difference between forgetting and forgiving. Often, I find that I don't forgive as much as I just forget. One is just allowing time to pass and a memory to get buried. The other is a conscious, spiritual release.

Forgiving someone doesn't mean that God doesn't intimately know and care about the pains I've experienced, or that He Himself won't hold my offenders accountable for what they have done. It simply means that I am releasing them, (and, in the process, releasing myself of the bondage of unforgiveness) in humble recognition of the debt I've also been forgiven.

"Freely you have received, freely give," Jesus said in Matthew 10:8. May those words mark the way we live—and forgive.

Celebrating the blessings of obedience,
Rachel

- 26 -
holiness:
sacred business

Since we have these promises, dear friends, let us purify
ourselves from everything that contaminates body
and spirit, perfecting holiness out of reverence for God.
2 CORINTHIANS 7:1

Dear Erin,

We live in a world full of pollutants, full of things that
stand opposed to God and His ways. Depending upon the
state of our hearts, these things either revile us or subtly
appeal to us.

Paul admonishes us to, "Hate what is evil and cling to
what is good" (Romans 12:9). Yet sometimes, like the Israelites who adopted the idols of the people around them, we
take the very things that God hates and give them prominent places in our lives. Without realizing it, we take things
born of the world's sinful values and adopt them as our own.
Although we never set out to dishonor God, we become

deeply intertwined with the culture around us and feed on its contaminants.

Our holy God wants those who serve Him to be holy as well (Leviticus 19:2). Obviously none of us can truly be holy apart from the cleansing blood of Christ. But once we are clothed with His forgiveness and purity, He wants us to keep striving for holiness "out of reverence" for Him. We dishonor Him whenever we grieve His Spirit and knowingly interface with sin (Ephesians 4:30).

A lot of things can contaminate our bodies and our spirits. Some we have already talked about: things like immodesty, bitterness and unforgiveness. There are many more contaminants we could talk about. But, for now, I want to address one that sticks out in my mind as a common "holiness pitfall" for many of us in this day and age: the area of media.

I'm not one to say that a Christian should never watch a movie or download a popular song. But I do believe that a lot of the things we allow our eyes to see and our ears to hear show not only a lack of reverence for God, but a love for the world and its ways.

I have known Christian women who, in addition to serving in various capacities at church, hate to miss an episode of "Sex and the City." And I've been to Christian weddings where the ceremony was full of worship songs, while the reception was full of the latest top 40 hits, many of which reflected morals and attitudes that stood in stark contrast to the Word of God. I can't help but see the dichotomy and wonder if we've lost touch with what it means to pursue holiness.

"Do not love the world or anything in the world," we are

told in 1 John 2:15. "If anyone loves the world, the love of the Father is not in him."

If we are truly able to feed on the things of the world, if we feel comfortable with and are entertained by them, what does that say about our understanding of and our reverence for a holy God? Furthermore, what of the scriptural command to feed our minds on that which is true, noble, right, pure, lovely, admirable, excellent or praiseworthy (Philippians 4:8)? Do we have any reverence for that instruction?

I'm not here to give any hard and fast rules. I personally find the need for constant reliance on and sensitivity to the Holy Spirit in this area. But I do want to encourage you to prayerfully examine your media diet and ask Him to show you any way in which it grieves His Spirit. Stay immersed in God's Word so that you can distinguish between right and wrong as you make choices (Hebrews 5:14). And keep in step with His Spirit, turning from anything that you sense is dishonoring to Him.

James tells us that the kind of religion God accepts as "pure and faultless is this: to look after orphans and widows in their distress and to keep oneself from being polluted by the world" (James 1:27). If we can keep those things in mind and pursue them, we'll be aiming for the right goal: becoming more like Jesus out of love and respect for who He is.

Warmly,
Rachel

The Heart
for personal reflection or group discussion

1. Describe one or two people you know who beautifully exemplify one of these quality traits.

2. How have you seen God at work in your life in one of these areas?

3. Which character quality in this chapter stood out as one you would like to strive for more of and why?

Recommended Resources

Absolute Surrender by Andrew Murray
In this devotional classic, Murray shows how we open the doors to abundant blessings by giving ourselves fully to God as living sacrifices. Touches on topics such as humility, the Holy Spirit, the power of complete trust and more.

Revolution of Character: Discovering Christ's Pattern for Spiritual Transformation by Dallas Willard with Don Simpson
By examining various aspects of our being–our heart, soul, mind and body–the authors examine how genuine spiritual transformation takes place.

The Release of the Spirit by Watchman Nee
A book that many have found absolutely life-changing. It may just transform the way you look at the Christian life.

Choosing Gratitude: Your Journey to Joy by Nancy Leigh DeMoss
Learn to be intentionally mindful of God's incredible gifts–and thus not allow Satan to steal your joy–by making the choice to live with a thankful heart.

Choosing Forgiveness: Your Journey to Freedom by Nancy Leigh DeMoss
Through Scripture, DeMoss shows that forgiveness is a choice and our only path to obedient, free living in Christ.

The Goodness of God: Assurance of Purpose in the Midst of Suffering by Randy Alcorn
Grow in your trust and understanding of God as Alcorn, who has endured much suffering himself, explores God's loving and higher purposes in the pain and tears of life.

PART III

The Home: serving your family

Her children arise and call her blessed;
her husband also, and he praises her:
"Many women do noble things,
but you surpass them all."
PROVERBS 31:28-29

We've looked at some of the life habits that help us abide in Christ and bear the fruit He wants us to bear. We've also looked at the "wellspring of life," our hearts, and how our character ought to increasingly reflect His likeness.

And where does this "wellspring" have one of its greatest spill-over effects? You guessed it—in our homes. For better or for worse, this is where our true character is most evident. Yet because we are so "on display" in our homes around the clock, it is also one of the places where we can make our biggest impact for Christ. In faithfully serving our families, we have a huge opportunity to bless God's heart and shape lives for His service.

May you be encouraged to pursue just that in the following pages.

- 27 -
being a builder

*A wise woman builds her house,
but with her own hands a foolish one tears hers down.*
PROVERBS14:1

Dear Erin,

You've probably heard it said, "If mamma ain't happy, ain't nobody happy." Aside from the poor grammar, I think there is a nugget of truth in this saying. As women, we are largely responsible for shaping the tone of our homes, setting the backdrop for the upbuilding we are called to do.

Author and speaker Renee Ellison puts it this way.

A mom's ongoing, running commentary is as vital to the success and atmosphere of the home as the very air that the family breathes. It is spiritual oxygen to the home, even if they live in a dark, dank basement in shantytown in a third world country. A mother can make a veritable heaven of any home simply by the choice of her words...She shapes reality for the entire family via her tongue.

Have you ever been in a home (or maybe you grew up in one) where the woman of the house was always down about something and exuded an overall spirit of despair? Or how about a home mothered by a woman with a critical, nagging tone, coupled with harsh outbursts of anger? Nothing ever seemed pleasant, much less joyful and enriching. That type of atmosphere can be oppressive for everyone around.

On the other hand, perhaps you have experienced life around a woman who was uplifting and kind, encouraging and cheerful, compassionate and patient, hospitable and helpful. No "walking on eggshells" required. If you're like me, this is the kind of woman you love to be around. In fact, this is the kind of woman you want to be! This woman knows how to build a house. The other one foolishly tears down the very thing she is supposed to be constructing.

What is your normal tone around the house? Do you exhibit joy? Do others feel at ease around you? Do they feel deeply valued and cherished? Do they feel delighted in?

Would your husband use the words, "cheerful, encouraging, and respectful" to describe you? Or would the words more likely be "grumpy, nagging, and worried"?

If we're honest, most of us have moments in both arenas: moments of building up as well as moments of foolishly tearing down. But, oh, how we must strive to be "builders" if we intend to be a godly influence in our homes. Oh, how we'd better strive to stay in the "building up" arena if we expect to leave a lasting legacy of abundant fruit to God's glory through our ministry to our husbands and children.

Nagging will never benefit our husbands or kids (Proverbs 21:9). Criticism and a spirit of dissension will never motivate them to soar to greater heights in Christ. No, the wise woman chooses to be a life-giver to her family by interceding for them, encouraging them and regularly breathing uplifting words.

Sure, there may be times when solemn things need to be spoken or discipline needs to be carried out, but even still those should be moments that build. "Reckless words pierce like a sword, but the tongue of the wise brings healing" (Proverbs 12:18). No matter what the mood or circumstance, always seek to let your words be "a tree of life" (Proverbs 15:4).

Cherish cheerfulness. Promote praise. Exude comfort.

You may even find it helpful to try setting small, measurable goals that will help you use your tongue for good at home. If you struggle with complaining, make it a point not to complain this month! If you struggle to be an encourager, aim to say two encouraging things to your husband and kids each day this week.

In addition to the words we use and the tone we set in the home, there are many other ways in which we can choose to be home builders: prayerfully planning out our days, knowing what's for dinner, spending focused time with our husbands, etc. I once made a list of all the things that I did that "built up" our home, as well as the things that worked to "tear down," such as procrastination, rushing/being late, and loose spending. Try making your own list and then put it in your Bible or somewhere else where you will see it regularly.

Regardless of where we may stand as "builders," let's remember that it is the Holy Spirit who will empower us to build. How desperately, then, must we rely on and stay connected to Him!

Blessings in the construction zone,
Rachel

I've Got a House to Build

by Rachel Thompson

Why do I strive for discipline
Why do I rise before dawn
Because I've got a house to build
And only one Foundation to build on

Can't start the day out of step with His Spirit
In hurry or scurry or noise
Must get alone in the quiet place
And hear the Savior's voice

For little lambs are depending on me
To shepherd them through the day
So I, too, must sit at the Shepherd's feet
Or I will lead them astray

And countless millions are living apart
From the One who alone can save
So I must let Him shape my mind
And burden my heart to pray

I need Him to form His image in me
I need to be Spirit-filled
This, my greatest necessity
For I've got a house to build

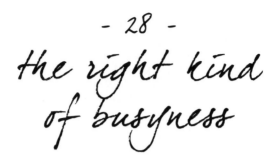

- 28 -
the right kind of busyness

*She watches over the affairs of her household
and does not eat the bread of idleness.*
PROVERBS 31:27

*We hear that some among you are idle.
They are not busy; they are busybodies.*
2 THESSALONIANS 3:11

Dear Erin,

The above verses imply that we are to have an agenda in our homes and be busy going about it.

The problem is that many women do not have a well-thought-out, godly agenda when it comes to their personal lives, their home, and the way they will help their family make a meaningful impact on the rest of the world.

Before you laugh at the idea of anyone being idle in this day and age (doesn't everyone seem crazily busy?), keep in mind that idleness does not always equal doing nothing. *It equals doing nothing productive.*

Idleness can mean frittering away time at home or it might mean being endlessly on-the-go. In either case, it means being involved in a host of things unattached to any lasting, valuable purpose or Spirit-led call.

We live in a day and age where it is not hard to fill up the calendar. Sometimes what keeps us hopping is pressure from others or making commitments to "good things" that are not necessarily what God wants for us. A dear mentor of mine used to say, "Not every need is a call." We may not even realize it, but when we commit to things lightly and fail to take firm steps based on seeking His counsel, we suffer and those around us suffer as well (1 Timothy 4:16).

Michael and I try not to take lightly the shaping of our days and calendars. And we've realized that what's needed before we can really make decisions about what we will and won't do with our time is a clear understanding of our priorities. What all are we actually trying to accomplish in life? What do we value most? Does our agenda line up with God's agenda? And does this activity or commitment help us achieve the bigger picture?

Author and Bible teacher Nancy Leigh DeMoss says:

> The question is not, "Are we living by priorities?" because we all live by some set of priorities. The question is, "Are we living by the right priorities? Are we living according to God's priorities for our lives and for our use of time? Are we being purposeful and intentional in the way that we spend our time?"

Meaningless busyness sets a pace that hinders God's peace, order and Spirit from ruling our hearts and our homes. It crowds out His voice and the things on His heart. And sadly, it prevents us from growth and having a meaningful, kingdom-building focus.

It's also important to distinguish truly purposeless activities from things that may only seem that way. Some women get discouraged by the monotonous tasks that often fill up their lives, such as cooking, cleaning, toddler-chasing, or grocery shopping. These tasks can easily feel void of meaning if we just take them at face value. But if we see them in the bigger light of serving our husbands and children as unto the Lord, they take on great worth!

Ultimately, a wise woman chooses activities and sets a pace that allows her to look after the most important things in life: fearing the Lord, meeting the needs of her husband, faithfully raising her kids in the Lord, and having a heart to help those outside her own family as well (Proverbs 31:30; 31:12; 31:20; 31:26; Deuteronomy 6:6-9; I Timothy 5:9).

Yes, her life is full and busy. But it is a godly, balanced, purposeful busyness, full of good fruit. May our kind of busyness be just as sweet.

With love,
Rachel

- 29 -
order in the home

For God is not a God of disorder but of peace.
1 CORINTHIANS 14:33

Dear Erin,

Have you ever noticed that some people are naturally in-clined toward order, while others struggle to achieve it? Some people can't stand to live without things being "just so" while others have no idea how to get them that way! Perhaps you are a person for whom this has not been an issue, but let me con-fess that for me it has been a huge struggle.

Sure, I like it when things are neat. I like it when the fridge is clean and the bathroom counter is clear. I like it when I can see the top of my desk and the bottom of the kitchen sink. It's just that achieving and maintaining those things does not come naturally to me!

But as I've grown in Christ, I have come to appreciate and value order so much more than I used to, for I've come to see that God Himself is a God of order. We see it in the world He made: orderly seasons, orderly days. We see it in the Scriptures: plans and patterns, intricate details.

Yes, as much as I can be willy-nilly about things at times, I see that God is structured. And if I want to be more like Him, I need to become more orderly myself.

I used to think becoming more organized was next to impossible. But the more I've pondered it, prayed about it, and worked toward it, the more He has begun to change me in this area. One of His biggest gifts has simply been giving me a desire for order. Even if I don't always attain to it with perfection, I'm still pressing on in that direction (Philippians 3:12).

I like to think of order in two categories: internal and external. Internal order has to do with the disciplines and habits that feed the soul and foster a heart of peace: our time in the Word, in prayer, in thinking through our priorities, and in planning our days. External order has to do with our surroundings and the routines that keep the home humming. The first is the most essential kind of order, but it tends to go hand in hand with the second.

The biggest thing that order does in our hearts and homes is to create a sense of peace. Cluttered minds and chaotic households often do the opposite. They make us too distracted to live quiet, prudent, and prayerful lives (I Peter 4:7).

Another benefit of order is time. You don't have to waste precious minutes looking for things you can't find. You don't have to make extra trips to the store because you didn't take the time to plan your menu or combine your errands. You don't always have to be late because you can wisely think through what it will take to get out the door before it's time to actually leave. (Unfortunately, I repeat that error far too often!)

Order also promotes health. Well-planned out meals are often healthier than grabbing something to eat on the go. Exercise can be built into a day with a little planning and discipline, even if it's just 10 minutes of floor exercises or lifting a few hand weights.

Order can even save you money! No late fees for forgetting to pay bills on time. No losing library books or forgetting their due dates. No having to pay for overnight shipping because you didn't get that present in the mail ahead of time. No having to order in food because you didn't get something in the crock pot for that day you got home right before dinner. Yes, order can save a lot of money.

Years ago, when God was just helping me to gain a new appreciation for this whole idea of being orderly, I made a list of words comparing order and its opposite.

For chaos I wrote down:
- frazzled
- late
- overwhelmed
- Where did I put my...
- Sorry I missed your birthday
- I wish I hadn't said yes to...

For order I jotted down:
- peace
- ahead of time
- prepared
- rhythm
- predictable
- neat
- efficient
- productive
- I've prayed about it and I've decided to...

No matter what my natural bent was, when I looked at those two lists, I decided that I wanted the latter one to describe how I lived. And I wanted it to describe how my children lived. (My, how my poor habits easily pass down to them!) Striving for victory in the area of order has become not only a personal goal, but a family value and something in which the kids are expected to help.

If orderly skills don't come naturally to you, don't worry. Pray about one or two areas to focus on for starters. Read a book on home organization to get some practical ideas. Come up with a month-long menu of your family's favorite meals. Read a good blog on house cleaning tips. Figure out the best way to manage your time and tasks with a day planner or digital device. Post checklists or spreadsheets that you find helpful.

Whatever you do, if you struggle in this area ask for God's help. Just because we are talking about junk drawers and cleaning routines doesn't mean we can achieve change on our own. Becoming like Christ in His orderliness is a spiritual process that will require humility, dependence, discipline and obedience. As someone still growing in this area, I cheer you on in the process!

Waving my pom poms,
Rachel

On Being a Wife

- 30 -
the calling of a wife

*The LORD God said, "It is not good for the man to be alone.
I will make a helper suitable for him."*
GENESIS 2:18

Dear Erin,

We've been talking about the home. In my next few letters, I want to look at the sacred relationship that God designed to be the foundational building block for our homes and families: marriage.

So exactly what was His purpose in creating marriage? More specifically, what is His calling to wives? Why did He create Eve and give her to Adam?

When we start with God's original intent for making woman in Genesis 2:18, two things stand out to me. First, the wife was created as a companion, a friend. It wasn't good for Adam to be alone. Secondly, she was created to be his helper.

Modern-day feminists find this premise insulting. And where this ungodly thinking has crept into the church, some Christian women find it insulting as well. Yet if you ask women who have embraced their God-given role, you will find testimony after testimony that speaks to the joy and fulfillment in God's perfect plan.

We can feel confident that if we embrace our calling as wives, we are not going to waste away internally, "lose our identity" and have no outlet for our talents. Rather, we will find the Scriptural principle to be true that the more we "lose our lives" in loving and serving another, the more we will find them (Mark 8:35). Yes, the more we embrace God's ways—including His ways in marriage—the more blossoming and blessing we will experience.

We live in a day and age where being a "leader" is touted as something to which we should all somehow aspire. Leadership books and seminars abound. But not many people talk about being "helpers." I think it is one of life's most underrated responsibilities!

Being a helper means you get to walk in the footsteps of Jesus, who didn't come to be served, but to serve (Mark 10:45). He didn't come to exert authority or lord it over anyone. He came to wash feet and die to the glory of God. That is the high and holy calling of a helper.

Being your husband's helper means you are on an assignment from God to help him discover and live out who God created him to be. It means you get to intercede for him. It means you get to be his number one encourager in life. It means you get to be his friend and intimate confidant.

It doesn't matter if he is the most godly man you know or if he has yet to even know God. The point is that you, by your actions, service, prayers and example can be the most life-giving human influence in his life.

Learn to cherish your role as a wife. It's not a restrictive role, but one from which you can blossom in scads of ways and bear all kinds of spiritual fruit according to the talents, passions and circumstances God has placed in your lap.

One last thing I love about God's marriage design is the way it can serve to intensify our friendship with Him. He is our heavenly husband, after all, and our earthly marriages can definitely serve to sweeten our intimacy with Him. Even our husband's imperfections can feed our friendship with God, reminding us of God's perfection and sole ability to meet our every need.

For example, when we feel misunderstood, we can know that God understands us in full. When we feel somehow wounded, we have a God who can comfort, heal and enable us to forgive. And when we need to pour out our hearts, we have a God who will not tire of listening to every nuance and detail. Yes, when our imperfect spouses somehow leave us lacking, we can experience the complete sufficiency of God to fill up our every need.

So revel in this thing called marriage. It is not a man-made idea, but a God-inspired one with a God-breathed blueprint that, when followed closely, will ultimately draw us closer to the One who wants intimate oneness with us.

Embracing the call,
Rachel

as to the Lord: submitting to your husband

Wives, submit to your husbands as to the Lord. For the husband is the head of the wife as Christ is the head of the church, his body, of which he is the Savior. Now as the church submits to Christ, so also wives should submit to their husbands in everything.
EPHESIANS 5:22-24

Dear Erin,

These verses have perhaps caused more controversy or offense than any other instruction relating to Christian marriage. Somehow, in our independent and sinful spirits, we don't like to be told to submit to anyone. We don't like to be told that someone is "head" over us.

Yet, as in all of nature, there are God-ordained laws in place that govern things and make them work (Jeremiah 33:25). One of these laws is the law of leadership. Churches, organizations and governments cannot operate well without a leader. And neither can families.

God is the one who has established an authority structure within the home and has made the husband the head. Because God and His ways are perfect, there is something beautifully perfect in this design—something we can only know by yielding to it.

Within marriage, God's ordained leadership structure serves as a living example of His relationship with us, of Christ's relationship to His bride. God is not asking us to submit to our husbands as a helpless people submit to a cruel dictator. He is asking us to submit to our husbands as the Church submits to Christ: willingly, out of love.

Submission is an act of worship—not to our husbands—but to the One who laid down His life in selfless service for us. The issue, then, has nothing to do with whether our husbands are "worthy" of our yielding to them at a particular moment. Rather, it is a matter of if we are going to submit to our husbands "in everything" as if to Christ Himself (Ephesians 5:24).

We may not always agree with or understand God's will, but we must submit to it. In the same way, we must yield to our husbands even when we don't see eye to eye with them because the greater issue at hand is our obedience to God.

I can think of several instances where, had it been up to me and not Michael, I would have decided differently on a matter. Yet, many times I've seen the wisdom of his view after the fact and am so glad I let him make the call. Even when it's not so clear, I can be at peace and find freedom in knowing that I submitted to my husband out of obedience to God.

When a husband lives out his role according to God's

perfect design, modeling his leadership after Christ, it is truly a beautiful thing. In the same way, the woman who understands God's authority structure and willingly submits to her husband as the head of their home is a rare and precious jewel.

Yet what about when God's blueprint is not closely followed? What is a wife to do, for instance, when her husband fails to be the godly leader he ought to be?

First, she must relentlessly hang onto, trust, and obey what God says. His ways are so perfect that they are always right—no matter what the situation or circumstance. Her need for grace, wisdom, and reliance on God is great, but in Christ she can still soar and experience victory.*

If her husband is passive, she should be careful to never take over the role she feels he is abdicating. Not only will this belittle him, but when overrun by his wife, a husband will likely never rise to be the man she wishes he was. Rather, a woman frustrated by her husband's lack of leadership or spiritual maturity should not underestimate the power of God to transform him. She should cooperate with God by striving to respect, encourage and honor her husband, while earnestly praying for him to become all God wants him to be.

If her husband is an unbeliever, she should also take a serious look at 1 Peter 3:1-6, where we see that a submissive wife can have an enormous impact on her man. God can use her quiet approach of a pure and reverent life as a testimony to her husband, winning him over "without words." This principle can even apply to a believing husband who is not walking with Christ as he ought. The Holy Spirit can bring conviction upon him through the quiet, godly example of his wife.

Now what about when the hindrance to God's perfect leadership design within the home is rooted not in the husband's failure to lead, but in the wife's resisting his authority?

Take a wife who shops unwisely, for instance, spending more than her husband wishes she would. Perhaps he has tried to talk to her about it. She knows what he wants and what the budget says, but she fails to adhere. He might put his foot down. But be careful—he also might let it go rather than confront a woman who doesn't seem to respect him anyway. By her lack of submission, he has already been humiliated and will quietly bow out of trying to do any more leading.

If you want to be a genuinely submissive wife, be careful to defer to your husband, giving him the honor he deserves. Sure, you can offer your insights as well, and he will likely appreciate hearing your wisdom on a matter, but share your thoughts with respect, in the right setting, and with a willingness to let him have the final say. You may be surprised to find a quiet strength and leadership ability emerge when you are careful not to step into your husband's God-given place.

Lastly, don't automatically envy your husband just because he has been given authority. Leaders, including our husbands, carry a weighty responsibility before God that I have often been glad I don't have to bear. Pray for your husband to be found faithful in the job of leading your family well!

Until next time,
Rachel

*(As an aside, it is worth mentioning here that wives in extreme cases need to know that godly submission does not mean submitting to physical abuse.)

- 32 -
from the heart: loving your husband

...Then they can train the younger women
to love their husbands and children.
TITUS 2:4

Dear Erin,

One of Michael's favorite questions to ask me is, "Do you still like me?"

He says it in a silly sort of way, waiting for me to assure him that yes, I do still like him. But I think his question reflects a deeper desire that we all have: we all want to know that we are special and that someone treasures us. Your husband is no different.

Does he know that you love him? Does he know that he is special to you? Does he know that his wife doesn't just take his existence for granted but treasures the time she gets to spend with him? *How* does he know these things?

You've likely heard about the man who told his wife

he loved her and that if anything ever changed he'd let her know. While humorous, this anecdote serves as a good reminder that it's important for us to express our love verbally. We can't just assume our husbands know how we feel about them. And even if they do, it is such a boost for them to hear it from us! Let your husband know that if he's got any friend in this world, anyone with whom he is totally safe, anyone who is cheering him on to true greatness in life, it's you.

But what if the reason your husband doesn't hear a lot of "I love you's" is because you're not exactly sure that you do? Maybe you have built up some pretty serious resentment against him. Maybe he doesn't make you feel very loved. Maybe he has broken his vows. Maybe he hasn't provided for your family. I've been around the block long enough to realize that these scenarios are very real for a whole lot of women.

I don't presume to have a quick fix, or to even begin unpacking some of these weighty issues here. The only thing I will say, with heartfelt compassion, is this: no matter what our situation, our model for loving our husbands is the same and it is Jesus Himself. "Love each other as I have loved you," He told his disciples in John 15:12.

As we reflect on Christ's selfless and sacrificial love, we gain insight into how He calls us to love—a love that might cost us deeply, even as it cost Him. The good news is that we don't have to manufacture this kind of supernatural love ourselves. The Holy Spirit is able it empower it in us as we abide in Him and obey His commands.

Connie Hultquist shares a remarkable testimony about her husband, who continually deserted her and her children and repeatedly ended up in jail. Rather than hardening her heart to her unbelieving spouse, she committed to loving him unconditionally. She always set a place for him at the head of the table, wouldn't let the kids bad mouth him, and whenever he would come back home, she would shower him with love:

> I'd bring him in the house, give him dinner, and speak peace and rest to him. I'd run the bath water for him to wash and feel like a man again. Compassion would rise up in my heart. I had the Lord, and my Jim didn't. I would reverence and praise him. (See the *www. aboverubies.org* article, "Bring Him Home.")

How awesome to see God's ability to empower supernatural love go beyond theory to reality. Jim did indeed become a believer and went on to be a loving husband and father for over 25 years before his death in 2005. Connie reflects:

> Our love and life together was the most gut-wrenching experience I ever had, but it was a one of a kind marriage. Would I do it all again? Yes, I would. Oh yes, it was worth it all. My marriage was tried in the fires many times, but I came out with a testimony of love and truth. My marriage has a message, "If you don't give up, you will see the glory of God."

The Gift of Intimacy

Loving our husbands not only involves loving them through faithfulness, service and words, but it also involves loving them through physical intimacy, a God-given gift with implications even in the spiritual realm.

"So they are no longer two, but one flesh. Therefore what God has joined together, let no one separate" (Mark 10:8b-9).

I am not a male, but I have gathered that for a husband, rejection or starvation in the bedroom is a significant stumbling block to his feeling loved by his wife. In God's design, once a husband and wife unite in marriage, they belong to each other.

"The wife's body does not belong to her alone but also to her husband. In the same way, the husband's body does not belong to him alone but also to his wife" (1 Corinthians 7:4).

Taking this passage to heart will definitely affect the way we view the physical aspect of our marriage. Our bodies are not ours to withhold. They belong to our husbands as well!

"Do not deprive each other except by mutual consent and for a time, so that you may devote yourselves to prayer. Then come together again so that Satan will not tempt you because of your lack of self-control" (1 Corinthians 7:5).

Physical intimacy is a gift that we have the responsibility to give to each other and, once again, something we can be supernaturally empowered to do. Remember Connie Hultquist, the wife whose husband continually left her and ended up in jail? Want to know how she felt about loving her husband physically? Connie says:

> No matter what he had done to me, we were still one flesh. He was my first and only husband—a terrible, ungodly, unfaithful husband, but he was still my husband. His healing came again and again as I forgave him and opened my love to him. I held nothing back.

Connie allowed herself to be a conduit of God's love to

her husband in the most intimate way.

Physically loving your husband may not be as costly as it was for Connie. Thankfully, intimacy can be both desirable and enjoyable. Yet, whether it's costly for us or not, we need to keep this in mind: just as God commands us to love Him with all of our heart, soul, mind and strength, so we should aim to love our husbands with our hearts, minds and bodies fully engaged and poured out—as unto the Lord. As with everything in life, let the gift of intimacy be an act of worship.

Drawing from His love,
Rachel

- 33 -

washing his feet: serving your husband

*Sitting down, Jesus called the Twelve and said,
"Anyone who wants to be first must be the very last,
and the servant of all."*
MARK 9:35

Dear Erin,

When you are a mother, you know very well what it's like
to be a servant. The day your infant is born, you begin working around the clock to meet his or her needs. You don't
expect it to be a "50/50" arrangement. You know very well
that your newborn has no ability whatsoever to serve you!

But what about with your husband? For most of us, our
expectations are a little higher—okay, maybe a lot higher.
Maybe we do expect things to be "50/50" in marriage.

Yet, once again with Jesus as our example, we note a
giving, not a taking, lifestyle. He didn't come to "break
even" with us. He came to outserve us 100%. "For even

the Son of Man did not come to be served, but to serve, and to give His life as a ransom for many" (Mark 10:45).

One of the biggest things that makes a marriage work is when both husband and wife are willing to outserve the other. But there are a few important things to keep in mind about this.

First, because of the different roles God has given men and women, and because of various personalities and talents, your service to your husband might not look exactly like his service to you. Just because you cooked on Monday, Tuesday and Wednesday doesn't necessarily mean he should cook on Thursday, Friday and Saturday. My husband, wonderful as he is, doesn't know a spatula from a frying pan! I have no notions of being served by him within the kitchen realm and that's okay with me. Your husband, on the other hand, might love to cook every chance he gets. Well, then receive his service with thanks! The point is, you may each excel in different areas and be best suited for certain roles as you serve each other. So be careful to avoid a tit-for-tat mindset.

Another thing to keep in mind is that a servant doesn't keep score. Service, in its purest form, has no return expectations. A servant doesn't serve in order to be served, nor serve only if he's served. He serves because he's a servant. That's just who he is. Even if your husband never lifted a finger to meet your needs, you still have the ability—and the calling—to serve him.

Strive to carefully meet his needs—big and little. Fight attitudes that say, "I'll let him fend for himself" or "He doesn't deserve it." Find ways to relieve burdens for him, making him feel loved and cherished. These are the little things that make you a joy and a delight in his eyes and in the eyes of the Lord!

Lastly, a true servant fights self-pity and bitterness. Remember the story of Mary and Martha? Martha scurried around making preparations for dinner while Mary sat and listened to Jesus. Martha got agitated. "Why am I doing all the work?" she thought. It's so easy for those little seeds of resentment to creep in. But when they do, we've usually got things all wrong.

Instead of serving "humbly in love" (Galatians 5:13) and receiving our reward from the Lord, we sometimes crabbily like to make it a point to let our husbands know how much our service is costing us.

Instead of being glad we can lighten our husband's load in some way, our own "Martha Syndrome" surfaces.

Instead of doing things "as unto the Lord", we do them for our husbands—so long as we are noticed and appreciated.

Oh, that we would recognize these roots of bitterness when they creep in and nip them in the bud! They are seeds of the enemy to sow discontent, steal our joy and rob us of pure acts of worship, fragrant offerings to the Lord.

May we draw from God Himself the ability to serve our husbands in a million different ways, blessing their hearts simply out of love. Because we serve a God who sees and repays in full, we'll never come up short!

Press on with joy,
Rachel

- 34 -

becoming his crown: honoring and respecting your husband

A wife of noble character is her husband's crown,
but a disgraceful wife is like decay in his bones.
PROVERBS 12:4

Dear Erin,

As wives, we can go down one of two roads. We can either grace our husbands like a beautiful crown, or we can become like a rotting abscess in their bones. One of the biggest determining factors in this is the level to which we honor and respect them.

Ephesians 5:33 says, "each one of you also must love his wife as he loves himself, and the wife must respect her husband."

Respect is crucial for a man. It gives him dignity. It makes him want to live up to it.

It's freeing to note that our husbands don't have to be respectable. We're simply told to respect them. And we don't have to decide if they are worthy of it. God is!

So we know our assignment, but what are some practical ways we can carry it out? How can we honor and respect our husbands in a way that will cause us to be an adorning crown to them? Here are a few things that come to mind.

First, prioritize your man. Let him know that he's not an afterthought! With a full house, I know how easy it can be to get wrapped up in the kids' needs or in my own to-do list that I don't make it a point to just stop and be with Michael. Focus communicates value. Don't let your husband get lost in the mix!

Secondly, protect his reputation. Determine not to talk negatively about him to others, even in a joking way. Is he good at certain things? Let people know about it—especially if he's around! As for his faults, no need to broadcast them. First Corinthians 13 reminds us that love "always protects."

Before going any further, let me add that there may be extreme cases where you need to confide in a godly friend or counselor in regards to something seriously troubling about your husband. If it is done prayerfully and for the long-term goal of building your husband or your marriage up—and not simply for the sake of griping—it likely does not fall in the spirit of what I am saying here.

Next, honor your husband in the eyes of your kids. If he has established some special house rules, see that everyone holds to them, even when he's not around. Talk respectfully to your kids about your husband and insist that they do the same. Build him up in their eyes!

Recently, my friend's 5-year-old daughter was at our

house for the afternoon. Somehow I overheard her saying to herself as she played, "I love my hub!" When I asked her what she meant, she said, "That's what my mom always says to my dad." Now there's a girl who is seeing this truth in action!

Another practical tip is to honor your husband's preferences. Is it important to him that when he comes home the house is in relative order and a meal is around the corner? Or does he like to pick up a knife and chop vegetables with you? Is it important to him that you don't make commitments or spend sizable amounts of money without first asking him? Is it bothersome to him when you bring up details needing answers right before bed? If you know anything that means a lot to your husband, do your best to honor it.

Lastly, speak respectfully to your husband. As you interact with him, especially if you aren't seeing eye to eye on something, be careful to still be gracious in your speech. Don't default to sarcasm or put downs. Don't raise your voice. Don't remind him of the last time you thought he had a bad idea. Don't undermine his God-given authority. By all means, talk it out and share your perspective, but be careful to communicate honor and a spirit of submissiveness.

Over the course of your marriage, make sure your husband gets one message loud and clear in this matter of honor and respect: "You may not be perfect, but I esteem you. I will treat you with dignity, extend grace for your faults and value you as my husband." Anything less than that will seem to him a whole lot more like decay than a crown.

Cheering you on,
Rachel

- 35 -
vitamins e and a: encouraging and appreciating your husband

But encourage one another daily, as long as it is called "Today,"
so that none of you may be hardened by sin's deceitfulness.
HEBREWS 3:13

Dear Erin,

Who doesn't need encouragement? Who doesn't thrive on words of affirmation? And who doesn't long to be appreciated—acknowledged and treasured for who they are?

I would argue that, as human beings, encouragement and appreciation are two of the greatest emotional needs we have. Perhaps that's why we are told to encourage each other–not every once in a while, but daily (Hebrews 13:3)!

As wives, one of our biggest jobs is to help our husbands fulfill their purpose in life: loving and serving Christ. That is hard to do apart from regularly speaking life-giving words.

In every role that he may have—Christ follower, husband, father, provider, friend—don't underestimate your potential to spur on your husband.

To encourage, by definition, means to inspire with courage. We all need to be infused with courage and confidence! The power of encouragement can often mean the difference between despair and perseverance, between throwing in the towel and victory.

The power of encouragement can often mean the difference between despair and perseverance, between throwing in the towel and victory.

I'm blessed to know this firsthand because I live with a man who is a great encourager. Not only does Michael often bless my days by saying things that make me feel valued, but he has also inspired me with the courage to do so many things I never would have attempted—much less finished—on my own. These letters, for instance, would have been dead in the waters of discouragement and weakness many times had God not used Michael to give me what I needed to press on.

While I don't consider myself a natural encourager, I've found many ways to encourage Michael as well—one of the biggest being the ministry of listening! A lot of times Michael needs to process thoughts or decisions by talking about them, even if I don't have a whole lot to add. It might be a new idea he has or a technical problem he's trying to work out in our recording studio. He just needs to talk it through and there is encouragement found when I'll just sit there and listen.

You perhaps don't realize the weight—and potential for encouragement–that your words and actions hold in your husband's life as well.

Is he feeling insecure about something? Maybe he just needs to know that you believe in him and that you will value him no matter what. Speak those words of encouragement to him.

Is he feeling taken for granted? Maybe he works hard to provide for your family. When is the last time you thanked him for being faithful in that? Verbalize your appreciation!

Did he do something helpful around the house? Or maybe a special favor for you? Make it a point to say thank you. Let him know it didn't go unnoticed!

Is he feeling tired and discouraged? If he's down, be the one to lift his spirits! Ecclesiastes 4:9-10 says, "Two are better than one…If one falls down, his friend can help him up." Breathe hope into him with truths from Scripture. Do something meaningful for him that might relieve some of his strain.

Does he need space? Give him the gift of some time alone—and let him know you'll take care of things so that he doesn't have to worry about them.

Is he unsure of his next step in a certain situation, or maybe in life? Be patient with him. Let him know you're praying for him.

In whatever way you sense that your husband needs to be lifted up, ask God to empower you to do just that. Many days, your simple and sincere words may be the only encouragement he gets and exactly what he needs to soar.

Here's to boosting your man,
Rachel

- 36 -
nagbusters: living peaceably with your husband

Better to live in a desert than with a
quarrelsome and ill-tempered wife.
PROVERBS 21:19

Dear Erin,

When you have kids, you will likely become very familiar with what nagging feels like. Kids can be very good at making their wants and needs known—sometimes with a little whine attached!

The dictionary describes nagging with terms like: "to scold, complain or find fault constantly" and "to be a constant source of anxiety or annoyance."

When put this way, it's no wonder that nagging our husbands is something we want to avoid at all costs. If our goal is to bring him good, not harm, all the days of our lives, nagging really cannot have a place in our marriages (Proverbs 31:12).

What does nagging do? First, it simply annoys. Remember when we talked about the choice between becoming our husband's crown or becoming like decay in his bones? Well, nagging definitely turns us into the latter. I don't want to be that, do you?

Nagging also belittles and devalues. When we're constantly finding fault with our spouse and expressing it, we are not honoring and respecting him like we should. We're just tearing him down, an unbecoming thing for someone designed to be a helper.

Lastly, nagging usually backfires. We might nag because we want this or because we're not happy about that. But very often, not only do we become as annoying as a dripping faucet (which we have in our kitchen right now, by the way, and it is very annoying!), but our husbands are not inclined to appease our nagging any more than we like to reward the nagging behavior of a whiny child.

Simply put, nagging is a bad idea. It doesn't accomplish anything good!

So how can we live peaceably with our husbands and steer clear of any hint of being quarrelsome or ill-tempered? How can we truly be crowns that grace their heads rather than thorns in their sides?

I think a lot of it goes back to the quiet and gentle spirit mentioned in 1 Peter 3.

Quarrelsome women strike up strife. Quiet and gentle women diffuse it.

Quarrelsome women demand what they think they deserve from their husbands, whether it be respect, an apology, or an action. Quiet and gentle women have another Source. And He is an infinitely marvelous One. When we feel wronged or misunderstood, there's no need to lash out at our spouse. No need to break the peace. Better to try humbly talking things out and hopefully coming to mutual understanding and reconciliation. But if we still feel wounded, we have a God who can shoulder the hurt and help us heal.

God sees and knows all (Genesis 16:13). He cares, and He invites us to pour out our hearts to Him (1 Peter 5:7; Psalm 62:8).

Yes, this is what separates a Christian marriage from one not in Christ. Ours is a cord of three strands and that third strand, Jesus Christ, makes all the difference. Two imperfect human beings do not have to find their full sufficiency in each other. They can each go to the One who is perfect. He can make up for every earthly shortcoming, absorb every sin and pain, and pour out the grace needed to fill up every crack and longing in their hearts. If your spouse is not a believer, he may not know this outside sufficiency, but Christ can still be all to you, allowing you to turn around and live in peace with your earthly love.

At the end of the day, I just encourage you to be sweet spirited with your husband, tender-hearted and full of forgiveness. Don't keep a record of his wrongs, nor harp on him about everything you wish he would do or become. Simply determine to live at peace with him, as far as it depends on you (Romans 12:18). In doing so, you will become a sweet aroma and a quiet, godly example to the man you love.

Blessings,
Rachel

power tool: prayer in marriage

Ask and it will be given to you; seek and you will find;
knock and the door will be opened to you.
MATTHEW 7:7

Dear Erin,

Did you know that God wants us to be characterized as askers? He wants us to request things of Him. Why? Because there are things on His heart He wants to do! And He has instituted this thing called prayer in order to set those things in motion. He wants us to invite Him into lives and situations to do great things according to His will—things that only He could do!

As married people, one of the key areas where our asking can be focused is toward our marriage and, in particular, our spouse. Before talking specifically about praying for your husband, let me mention praying for your marriage.

Have you ever noticed how aggressively Satan seeks to

attack and bring down marriages? Our enemy is a stealer, a killer and a destroyer, and the realm of marriage—Christian or not—seems to be one of his main targets. We must be found calling upon God's protection.

At our wedding rehearsal, a highly respected mentor of ours called Michael over to talk to him. "Will you make me a promise?" he asked. "Promise me that you and Rachel will commit to praying for your marriage every single day."

We've been married for twenty years now and that simple advice continues to have a daily—actually nightly—impact on us. See, every single night before we go to sleep, we lay in bed and pray briefly for our marriage. Among other things, we regularly ask Him to grow our love for one another, to keep our marriage pure and to protect us from the enemy's schemes. While we may not be able to tangibly measure the cumulative effect of those prayers, my strong sense is that God has heard, answered and blessed our requests over the years.

Whenever we attend a Christian wedding, we always give the couple the same advice we received—and I advise the same to you! Ask your husband if he would be willing to pray with you each day—at whatever time and in whatever way works best for the two of you. If, for some reason, your spouse is not comfortable praying with you, you can always commit to carrying the torch on behalf of both of you. Just commit to daily bringing your union and its needs before the One who has joined you together and has the desire and power to keep you together and cause you to flourish.

In addition to praying for your marriage, I encourage you to personally, specifically and faithfully pray for your husband. This is one of the most powerful ways you can "bring him good" all the days of his life! However much your husband desires God now, pray that his hunger for God would increase. Pray that he would "open his mouth wide" and that God would fill it (Psalm 81:10)!

Ask God to give your husband a soft, surrendered heart that desires to "bear much fruit." Ask Him to reveal to your husband any sin, greed or worldly ambition that may be lurking in him undetected. Pray for his sexual purity.

Pray for healing or deliverance from anything that has wounded him in the past or holds him in bondage. Ask God to speak into his life by His Word and His Spirit (Psalm 25:9).

Do you sense faults or see sins in your husband's life? Do you think he watch-

Have you ever noticed how aggressively Satan seeks to attack and bring down marriages? We must be found calling upon God's protection.

es too much TV? Do you see outbursts of anger? Do you wish he read his Bible more? Pray (don't nag!) regularly and patiently and watch for God to do His work. And ask God to give you the compassion, love and obedient heart you need to love your husband well despite these imperfections, while humbly remembering your own (Matthew 7:3).

Consider writing down key prayers for your husband's life on a sheet of paper that you keep in your Bible (or wherever you'll see it regularly) and pray prayers along those lines again and again, watching expectantly for God's answers and recording them when they happen (Psalm 5:3; Psalm 77:11)!

One great way to do this is to pick key passages of Scripture that you use to inform your prayers. Pray, for example, that your husband would be the kind of man described in 1 Timothy 3:1-3. Pray that he would be a faithful father according to Colossians 3:19 & 21.

To sum it all up, for as long as you are married, seek to nourish your marriage and your husband well through the essential ministry of prayer.

With love,
Rachel

On Being a Mom

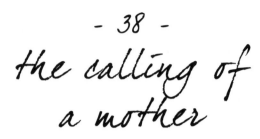

- 38 -
the calling of a mother

She speaks with wisdom and faithful instruction is on her tongue...
Her children arise and call her blessed.
PROVERBS 31: 26-28

Dear Erin,

When our kids are young, it's so hard to imagine that a day will come when they won't be around; the house will be quiet and the bedrooms will be empty. But it's true.

All in all, our kids will likely spend less than one fourth of their days in our home. That means that about 75% of their lives could be spent living out beliefs and values gained while under our influence. Parenting truly is a sacred trust.

As easy as it is to focus on the days at hand, as parents we need to think about the big picture from the beginning. What is our vision for our kids? What do we want them to look like when they leave our nest? What is our highest desire for their lives?

Will we be satisfied if they simply pay lip service to God? Or do we long for them to truly fall in love with Him above all else? Do we have a vision for them to shine like stars in a crooked and depraved generation as they hold out the Word of Life (Philippians 2:15-16)? Do we want them to be world changers? Or are we okay if they look an awful lot like the rest of their generation?

As Christian parents, if we don't do something drastically different than the rest of society in raising our kids, it is very possible that they, like many of the Israelite children, will become worshippers of the gods of the people they lived amongst.

That's why our job as parents, and especially as mothers, is so crucial. Who our children become and how they will impact others is largely shaped by the few years they spend with us. Our influence is huge and it has eternal ramifications.

So, in its simplest form, what exactly is a mother's calling? What is it that we, in conjunction with our husbands, are tasked with doing? I believe our bottom line responsibility boils down to one word: discipleship.

Discipleship is the process of passing down our faith with the goal of seeing others grow into mature followers of Christ.

That may seem basic. I mean, isn't that what naturally happens when parents are Christians—they bring their kids up to know God? Well, you would think it would be natural, but the reality is that training kids up in the fear and instruction of the Lord takes being extremely purposeful and diligent.

Many Christian parents who don't object to this calling also, perhaps unknowingly, fail to embrace it. You may be familiar with the Old Testament story of Eli the priest. Even though he held a high spiritual office in Israel, we are told in 1 Samuel that he had two sons who were terribly wicked—and they did their wicked deeds right at the Tabernacle! As the Bible goes on to talk about how these two behaved, it points the finger back at Eli and says that even though he knew what they were doing, "he failed to restrain them" (I Samuel 3:13).

Like Eli, many Christian parents have every intention of bringing up their children in the ways of God. They put them in Sunday School, try to model Christian lives and promote good Christian morals. Yet years down the road, many realize that there is a gap between *their* values and the values of their kids. There is a breakdown between the importance of the Christian faith in their lives and in the next generation. And they see in their kids an all-too-similar-to-the-rest-of-the-world lifestyle and mindset.

Looking at Scripture, what guidelines are we given for diligently passing on the faith to our kids? How can the season of shepherding our kids into adulthood be all God intended for it to be? I look forward to delving into some of these issues in my next few letters.

With love,
Rachel

- 39 -
imparting truth, instilling vision

*These commandments that I give you today are to be upon your
hearts. Impress them on your children. Talk about them when
you sit at home and when you walk along the road, when you
lie down and when you get up.*
DEUTERONOMY 6:6-7

Dear Erin,

When Deuteronomy 6 tells us to impress God's commandments on our children, notice it says they first have to
be upon our hearts. We can't pass on what we don't have!

Yes, when it comes to passing on a living and growing
faith to our kids, there is no substitute for having a vital
personal relationship with Christ ourselves. How we interact
with our kids and what we teach them will flow from our
own walk with Jesus.

That said, how do we actually go about passing on the

truths that are in our hearts to our kids?

Imparting Truth

First, we must remember that discipleship is not a matter of a few big moments, but little, daily deposits, year after year, that compound over time. God's desire for the Christian family is that from a child's earliest months and years, his parents are faithfully teaching the Word of God through countless conversations and settings. These things are the very lifeblood of the home. They mark a child's memory and shape his character.

In his classic parenting book, *Raising Your Children For Christ,* 19th century minister Andrew Murray said, "The entrance of divine truth in the mind and heart, the formation of habit and the training of character, are not attained by sudden and isolated efforts, but by regular and unceasing repetition."

With these thoughts in mind, there are countless things we can do to see to it that our kids are continually being taught truth. Here are just a few:

- Let them listen to an audio Bible when they're falling asleep at night
- Keep the radio off in the car and talk to them
- Read them inspiring, character-building stories
- Teach them Scripture songs while they're taking a bath
- Tell them something you learned during your devotions
- Allow them to interact with inspiring Christian adults
- Involve them in serving others
- Talk about how you see God in the world.

Personally, I love looking at things in the natural world and finding spiritual lessons. They are all over the place! In fact, Amy Carmichael called nature "the second bible." It really is true that "God's invisible qualities—his eternal power and divine nature—have been clearly seen, being understood from what has been made..." as Romans 1:20 says. So use that to imbed truths into your children. Show them how plants thrive near water and suffer

We have to get our kids to understand that they have been "saved to serve." They have a purpose and a mission!

when parched. Relate that to our need to be planted in God's Word, as seen in Psalm 1. Talk about how God is like a rock. Discuss the significance of a rainbow. Imagine with your kids how much power it would take to instigate lightning!

Your goal is that over time, your kids will begin to look at life through the lens of Scripture. They will recognize God's handiwork in creation, be able to discern between right and wrong, and know how to make wise decisions.

Instilling Vision

We also need to help our kids understand their God-given reason for being. We need to help them grasp that they were saved for more than a "happily ever after" existence. God's ultimate goal for them is that they know Him and bear much fruit to His glory.

When God brought the Israelites out of Egypt, their redemption was not an end in itself. God wanted to put that nation on display for the rest of the world to see. They were to be His instruments for the redemption of all who would believe in Him.

We have to get our kids to understand that they have been "saved to serve," as Andrew Murray puts it. They have a purpose and a mission!

The Apostle Paul wrote, "And he died for all, that those who live should no longer live for themselves but for him who died for them and was raised again." Our kids are not to live for themselves! They have been bought at a price. Life is not to be about their personal comfort or plans, but about His glory and His will. They must know that! Murray said:

> Let us devote every child to God and His service. Let us stop praying that our children will be saved if we are not willing to offer them for His service...The greatest dangers to Christ's Church are friendship with the world and the seeking of riches...Let us seek this one thing–that our children may become worthy and equipped to be set apart for the service of the King!

Is that our heart's desire for our kids? And are we modeling this life of service as parents?

See, over time, our children will come to understand what is most important to us. They will know what we really live for. They will see what we seek after the most. They will have a good idea about the nature of our devotional lives. They will know the value we place on prayer, on people and on possessions. They will know the level to which we care about the poor and the lost. They will know whether or not we really love God and love others. It's hard to hide who we really are during eighteen years of scrutiny!

In the end, of course, our children will still have to choose Jesus for themselves (Joshua 24:15). They will have to personally decide what their lives are going to be about. But we know that our job, with the help of the Holy Spirit, is to intentionally teach and model a God-centered, Kingdom-focused life.

That's the planting and watering we must do in our kids' lives as we pray for God to do what only He can do: make the seeds grow (1 Corinthians 3:6).

Relying on Him,
Rachel

Your Tender Lambs

by Rachel Thompson

The moments are fleeting
They are quickly passing by
And soon—before you know it
Your lambs will take off and fly

Will they soar with wings as eagles
Love the Lord with all their heart
Or will the world have gotten its grip on them
Because you didn't do your part

It is yours to disciple them
That's the job I've given you
Don't be fooled into thinking
You've got more important things to do

Seize the minutes and the hours
As the days turn into years
They love your full attention
Give it often, keep them near

The wolves will offer to take over
The job I've given you
So guard your tender lambs
Embrace what's yours to do

Let My Word live richly in you
So that you'll have things to say
As you sit at home with them
And as you walk along the way

Sow the Words of Life
Deep within their hearts
To guard their minds and light their way
For the days you'll be apart

Teach them they are not their own
I bought them at a price
I've a job for them to do
If they'll offer Me their life

Tell them there's no greater joy
Than walking in My ways
Inspire them by the way you live
To seek Me all their days

parental laziness

I went past the field of the sluggard, past the vineyard of the man who lacks judgment; thorns had come up everywhere, the ground was covered with weeds, and the stone wall was in ruins.
PROVERBS 24:30-31

Dear Erin,

One of the biggest causes of Christian parents failing to pass on the faith to their children is what Andrew Murray calls, "parental laziness." While I had never thought of the above verses as a passage on parenting, I believe we find here two key ways that Christian parents can be lackadaisical in their role.

Weeds on the Inside

The first type of laziness comes from the weeds and thorns we allow to grow "on the inside" of our kids' hearts and our homes. Because everyone is born with a sinful nature, often times our kids will act in ways that reveal the folly within them. These "inner weeds" can show up as anything from sibling bickering to defiance, from disrespect to lying.

As parents, it's easy to lack judgment and let these things

slide. But as we see in this passage, if we don't tirelessly pluck the plants of sin in the garden of our kids' hearts so they cannot linger and fester, their hearts will soon become overgrown with weeds and thorns.

"Folly is bound up in the heart of a child, but the rod of discipline will drive it far from him" (Proverbs 22:15).

Had King David taken this to heart, he might have saved himself much grief. Near the end of his life, his son, Adonijah, attempted to take the kingdom from his father. As he plotted the overthrow, we read, "His father had never interfered with him by asking, 'Why do you behave as you do?'" By letting Adonijah develop without consistently seeking to align his heart and actions with righteousness, David had dropped the ball as a parent. Adonijah had become a man who dishonored his father and his nation in a deplorable way.

Yes, like a garden left to itself, if not consistently taught, corrected and disciplined in a gentle and godly way, our children's hearts will become places where weeds and thorns abound.

Threats from the Outside

But weeds are not a garden's only threats. Enemies lurk from the outside as well. These can be the "foxes that ruin the vineyard" or the "thieves" that come in to steal, kill and destroy (Song of Solomon 2:15; John 10:10).

A gardener who is serious about his crops will do something to keep the bad guys out. So, too, a parent who is serious about parenting will ensure that the "stone wall" doesn't lie in ruins.

Let me start by saying that the first and most crucial "stone wall" that a parent must erect is that of prayer. Prayer, more than anything else, creates a supernatural covering over your child's life. It is not the only thing you must do, but it is the most important.

In addition to praying for our marriage every night before we go to sleep, Michael and I have made it a habit to pray for our kids. We pray not only for things like physical safety, but also for God's hand to be upon their lives, shaping their minds, capturing their hearts to do His will, and protecting them from the schemes of the enemy. Yes, what a crucial aspect of being guardians is the ministry of praying for our kids. I encourage you to make it a daily priority.

With prayer as the foundation, what "foxes" and "thieves" do we need to guard against in order to maintain a strong stone wall around our kids' lives? Well, the vices come in all shapes and sizes. Any of them can threaten to work against what we are trying to do as we disciple our children.

One looming enemy I want to touch on in particular is friendship with the world. James 4:4 says that anyone who chooses to become a friend of the world becomes an enemy of God. We are a people called to be set apart! But how many youth from Christian families end up being so influenced by worldly peers and worldly media that there is virtually no distinction left—in thought, dress, belief or behavior. While believing parents may not intend it to be so, their impact can become easily overshadowed by other influences if intentional steps to guard against this are not taken.

As Christians, we live in the world. We interface with non-believers all the time. And that's a *good* thing for people whom the Bible calls the "salt of the earth!" However, there is a big difference between our children interacting with non-believing peers and having their lives endlessly intertwined with them, especially if they are little intertwined with us. "He who walks with the wise grows wise, but a companion of fools suffers harm" (Proverbs 13:20).

Likewise, without careful parental oversight, our kids can easily be bombarded with messages from the god of this age through various forms of media. The Christian parent must relentlessly guard what goes into their children's hearts and minds, keeping in mind what is pleasing to God and the enormous impact that ungodly media can have. Do we expect our kids not to be negatively affected in their spirits when we allow them to read books, watch movies, listen to music or play video games saturated with disrespect, immodesty, violence, the occult or sexually immoral practices? Do we expect them not to be negatively affected when we allow them to feast on a Facebook page full of godless chatter by godless peers? We must stand on guard.

Lastly, note this: as we diligently tend to the garden of our kids' hearts and maintain a strong stone wall against outside threats, our focus shouldn't just be on playing defense against evil. It should also be to joyfully and practically teach our kids what it looks like to choose God's ways, walk in His righteousness and enjoy the blessings obedience brings.

With love,
Rachel

Ten Prayers for Your Children

by Rachel Thompson

May they have a different spirit and
follow You wholeheartedly (Num. 14:24)

May they be oaks of righteousness for the
display of Your splendor (Is. 61:3)

May they have a great love for the
Word of God (Ps. 112:1; Is. 66:2b; Ps. 119:65)

May they exhibit the fruit of the Holy Spirit (Gal. 5:22-23)

May You do the supernatural work of causing
the seeds planted and watered in them
to grow and flourish (1 Cor. 3:6)

May they not love the world or conform to its patterns,
but wholly devote themselves to serving You,
seeing their lives as nothing but a living sacrifice
(2 Cor. 5:15; Rom. 12:1-2; 1 Chron. 29:5; 1 John 2:15)

If they marry, may they marry spouses who are
equally set apart to You for Your purposes; may they
marry others who shine like stars in
their generation as they hold out the Word of Life
(2 Cor. 6:14; Php. 2:15-16).

May You protect them from the evil one and deliver them from any of his schemes, snares or fiery arrows (Mt. 6:13; John 17:15; 1 Pet. 5:8-9; Eph. 6:16)

May they bear much fruit in their lives to Your glory (John 15:8; Lk. 8:8)

May their hearts always be set on things above, eagerly awaiting the coming of Christ and longing for His appearing (Col. 3:1; Php. 3:20; 2 Tim. 4:8)

- 41 -
cultivating a quiet heart

The fruit of righteousness will be peace; the
effect of righteousness will be quietness and confidence forever.
ISAIAH 32:17

Dear Erin,

God calls us to lead peaceful and quiet lives. As parents,
one of the best things we can do for our kids is to help them
develop the inner life—the part of them that learns to reflect,
give thought to their ways, and listen to God's gentle and
quiet voice. They must learn to enjoy and seek out the "still
waters" of life, because these are vital to the nourishment
of the God-centered soul (1Peter 3:4; 1Thessalonians 4:11;
1Timothy 2:2; Psalm 23:2).

Quietness not only feeds the spiritual life of our kids,
but it helps bring to life all sorts of virtues and talents. It can
draw out the immense creativity within a child made in God's
image. It can encourage resourcefulness, imagination, thank-

fulness, patience and, in great measure, parent or sibling relationships.

Yes, a quieter home more naturally lends itself toward conversation and relationship, the basis of parental discipleship (Deuteronomy 6:7). Conversations that will impact a child's heart are harder to come by when there is a constant din of noise from the TV, computer or mp3 player, even if the content is decent.

Quietness truly is a gift to be seized. While things like media can be enriching, sometimes we let too much "noise" into our lives— noise that hinders many of life's greatest gifts.

While things like media can be enriching, sometimes we let too much "noise" into our lives–noise that hinders many of life's greatest gifts.

Ours is certainly not a TV-free household, but over the years we have chosen to keep TV/video watching at a minimum for the kids, especially during the daytime. We've also tried to keep any computer or game time minutes very limited (and have them be the first privileges to go when a punishment is needed for something!). This has less to do with the media content as much as it does with trying to cultivate the peace and quiet that encourage other godly virtues.

By the way, it can be easy to assume, "My kids don't take in that much media." But try keeping a log of all the media time they have in a week between TV, computer, video games, music and various hand held devices. You might be surprised to find out how many hours your child is actually spending doing something that is not quiet.

On the flip side, one form of media that we have encouraged a great deal is listening to audio recordings of the Bible. Faith Comes by Hearing has a great resource called *Kidz Bible*– roughly 300 tracks of audio, dramatized Bible stories right out of Scripture. (They have many adult Bible versions available on their site as well. Visit *www.faithcomesbyhearing.org.*)

Our kids have listened to audio Bible resources during naps and at bedtime for years and we have been amazed at what they have learned. When our oldest was about 9 years old, she suddenly realized that she could recite the whole genealogy of Jesus from Matthew chapter 1 by heart, all because she had heard it so many times!! I find the other kids quoting Scriptures or referring to Bible stories I didn't even realize they knew, all because of what they've heard over and over again while listening. So yes, this is one form of media we've been happy to let fill the airwaves around here!

Well, I hope these thoughts from my heart to yours will help shape the way you think about the tone and environment you want to set in your home. Harbor stillness, encourage the inner life and point your kids to the Word. This will serve you and your children well for the years to come.

Shhhhhhh,
Rachel

- 42 -
servants of all

Sitting down, Jesus called the Twelve and said,
"Anyone who wants to be first must be the very last,
and the servant of all."
MARK 9:35

Dear Erin,

I once heard someone say, "If you want your kids to be servants, don't treat them like royalty."

It's true that in wanting the best for their kids, some parents lay out such a red carpet lifestyle that their kids begin to think that the world revolves around them. This can happen not only through material abundance, but by building a family's schedule or focus all around the children. Without meaning to, parents can foster a habit of expectation, entitlement and selfishness by catering to their children's whims and wishes or by allowing their children's lives to be filled with activities that can feed pride and self-centeredness if left unchecked.

While we are to delight in our children and shower them with love, they also need to know that they fall within a greater framework and a grander purpose. Simply put, the world does not revolve around them! It revolves around the God of the universe, who wants and deserves their lives. Only in Him will our kids break free from the self-life and find their greatest joy and fulfillment.

Requiring Service

One of the best ways to combat selfishness is to require our children to serve. This can first be taught at home through regular, age-appropriate chores as they learn to contribute to what maintaining a home requires.

Household responsibilities should be at their level, but not below it. Requiring a fifth grader to simply make her bed each day and take out the garbage once a week is not the kind of thing that will get them into the habit of serving or thinking about others. Laurie Flem, mother of eight, wisely says, "Children older than age seven should be helping more than they require of you." Kids can do a lot more than you might think—and it is good for them!

We keep a checklist for each child of the daily chores they are responsible for (dishes, laundry, vacuuming, lawn mowing, etc.). Not only does it build discipline, but it also negates the expectation that we, as parents, are here only to serve them.

As your kids grow, see to it that they are not only serving within the home but outside of it as well. Guard against the self-indulgent lifestyle that our society expects and encourages in young people. Send them out to serve!

Is there a single mother in your church for whom your daughter could offer free babysitting? Or a busy mother of young kids for whom she could be a much-welcomed mother's helper? Is there an elderly couple down the street whose driveway your son could shovel when it snows? A marginalized peer they could reach out to or spend time with? Something they could help out with at church? How about encouraging your kids to learn about and pray for the persecuted by visiting a site like *www.kidsofcourage.com*? Ask the Holy Spirit to show you ways your kids might be able to meaningfully meet the needs of others in His name.

Inspiring Service

While we can certainly steer our kids into service by requiring it, it is worth noting that we also need to lead them into service by inspiring it. Who do they see us serving? Are there ways they can come alongside us and help? Are we showing them what a giving life looks like? Ultimately, if our kids see us joyfully pouring out our lives for Christ's sake, they are much more inclined to follow suit.

In addition to setting a personal example, make it a point to fill your kids' minds with exciting stories of Christians who have served throughout history. Read age-appropriate stories of great believers to them and, as they get older, supply them with captivating Christian biographies they can read on their own. Also let them personally interface with adults who lead inspiring, serving lives. I absolutely love it when our kids get to be around adults whose lives are a living testimony of what it means to love Christ by serving others.

Jesus said, "Greater love has no one than this: that he lay down his life for his friend" (John 15:13). I hope that your kids and ours leave the nest not only knowing this truth, but having hands and feet experienced in living it out.

With love,
Rachel

The Home
for personal reflection or group discussion

1. How do you think your husband or kids would describe your overall tone at home? In what ways would you like to grow or change in this area?

2. If you are married, how do you feel you are most God-honoring as a wife? What do you find most challenging?

3. If you have children, what are your main focuses at this stage in their lives to best help them know and walk in the truth?

Recommended Resources

The Power of a Praying Wife and *The Power of a Praying Parent* by Stormie Omartian
These best-selling books will teach you not only about the how and why of prayer, but also will equip you with Scripturally-based prayers to pray for your husbands and kids, covering nearly every conceivable aspect of their lives. God has used these books to save many a marriage and child!

The Meaning of Marriage: Facing the Complexities of Commitment with the Wisdom of God by Timothy Keller
By painting a biblical vision for marriage, Keller debunks much common, but errant thinking and inspires marital commitment through practical wisdom and insights.

Raising Kids for True Greatness: Redefine Success for You and Your Child by Tim Kimmel
Dismantling the world's view of success with all of its vanity, Kimmel gives parents tools to help their kids be truly successful in three crucial areas: choosing their mission, their mate and their master.

The Ministry of Motherhood: Following Christ's Example in Reaching the Hearts of Our Children by Sally Clarkson
A beautiful look at a mother's call to disciple her kids–lavishing them with the gifts of grace, faith and inspiration while instilling a heart to serve Him.

The Contemplative Mom: Restoring Rich Relationship with God in the Midst of Motherhood by Ann Kroeker
Wisdom and personal insights from a mom who learned to "live a life filled with reflective moments even in chaos."

PART IV

The Harvest: impacting your world

Then he said to his disciples,
"The harvest is plentiful, but the workers are few."
MATTHEW 9:37

The more we walk with Christ, the more we'll realize that our calling doesn't end with fostering our relationship with Him and faithfully ministering to the needs of our families. While those things are incredibly God-glorifying in and of themselves, the very nature of being His disciples means that He also wants us to be His witnesses—beyond our front doors and across the globe (Acts 2:8)!

Throughout the Bible, we see women used in God's great plan of redemption—certainly through the impact they had as wives and mothers, but also in things like reaching out to the poor and needy, providing hospitality, caring for orphans and widows, looking after the needs of God's servants, and participating in the proclamation of the gospel (Proverbs 31:20; 2 Kings 4:8; John 4:28-29; James 1:27; Philippians 4:3).

As I wrap up my thoughts on godly womanhood, I want to spend some time taking a brief look at what it means to be a "woman of the harvest," actively cooperating with God in His big picture plan to reconcile a lost world to Himself.

- 43 -

agents for His appeal

All this is from God, who reconciled us to Himself through Christ and gave us the ministry of reconciliation...We are therefore Christ's ambassadors, as though God were making His appeal through us.
2 CORINTHIANS 5:15-20

Dear Erin,

Each of us lives in a little world of our own, filled with the people we know and interact with on a daily basis. But take a step back with me for a few minutes. Let's remind ourselves of the bigger picture. Currently there are over seven billion people worldwide living in over 200 countries and speaking nearly 7,000 different languages!

David Platt, author of *Radical*, points out that roughly one-third of these people claim to be Christian, though many from only a cultural or political standpoint. At the very, very least, that leaves 4.5 billion people who remain estranged by sin from the God who created them. Without Christ, the Bible says they face eternity in a place called a "lake of fire" (Revelation 20:15).

Could there be a heavier thought? A more unsettling truth? A more staggering reality?

Some of these people are in our close spheres: our neighbors, our friends, our family. Others are people we've never met who live halfway across the world. God loved them all so much that He sent His only Son as a sacrifice for their sins, offering eternal life to any who would believe in Him (John 3:16).

But how will they know the message of John 3:16? How will they hear about this glorious gospel? How will the 4.5 billion and more learn that they must call on the name of Jesus and be saved?

In 2 Corinthians 5:20, we find the answer to this question: ordinary Christ followers like you and I need to tell them! "We are therefore Christ's ambassadors, as though God were making His appeal through us."

Those of us who, by God's grace, have been rescued from the "dominion of darkness" and brought into the "kingdom of light" have been tasked with the job of sharing the good news of His salvation with the world (Colossians 1:12-13). We've been given the ministry of reconciling lost people to God!

"As the Father has sent me, I am sending you" (John 20:21).

"But you will receive power when the Holy Spirit comes on you; and you will be my witnesses in Jerusalem, and in all Judea and Samaria, and to the ends of the earth" (Acts 1:8).

"Therefore go and make disciples of all nations, baptizing them in the name of the Father and of the Son and of the Holy Spirit…" (Matthew 28:19).

It couldn't be more clear that Jesus gave us this "Great Commission," as it is often called. It's not an optional add-on to the Christian life, but a lens through which we are to see our very existence.

A political ambassador lives in a foreign country with a crystal clear understanding of why he is there and whom he is representing. We are to live in this world in much the same way—not as people who feel at home here, but as those from another kingdom, living to be its fragrance and inviting others into its citizenship. That is our calling!

The Great Commission is not an optional add-on to the Christian life, but a lens through which we are to see our very existence.

But the Great Commission is more than just a calling. It's also a gift. It's God's gracious way of allowing us to participate in the most amazing and epic story ever–a story still heading for its historic climax, when people from every tribe and tongue on earth will be gathered around God's throne in Heaven declaring Him to be the Lamb of God, the King of Kings and Lord of Lords! It is the most joyful thing we could ever be a part of!

Your fellow ambassador,
Rachel

- 44 -
the high stakes of eternity

For wide is the gate and broad is the road that leads to destruction,
and many enter through it.
MATTHEW 7:13

Dear Erin,

Every day you see the people in "your world." You see them walking by your house. You see them in their cars on the road. You see them at the stores. You see them at offices and restaurants and ballgames.

But have you ever stopped to consider this: for everyone whom you see on a daily basis, whether they die "in Christ" or not is the single most important factor of their lives? Nothing else—nothing—will matter in the end. It can be easy to forget that ultimate reality.

A few months ago our family was driving down a Chicago highway on a hot, July day as we headed to a family reunion at Lake Michigan. The kids were all buckled in and having a great time as we headed down the road. I was enjoying that feeling of having finally finished all the last minute packing details and had my feet up on the dashboard as we drove. Michael was behind the wheel, treating us to some favorite family tunes as he drove.

As we zoomed along, we encountered a typical summer construction zone, but thankfully traffic was still sailing along smoothly enough. A little further down, we approached a fork in the road: to the left was an express lane with concrete slabs on either side, while the other lanes were more open with a normal shoulder off to the right. For a moment, Michael muttered out loud about which lane he should pick, but ended up just staying to the more spacious right lanes since traffic was moving along just fine anyway.

Well, soon "moving along just fine" turned into a lot of slowing down. And that soon turned into a standstill, which finally turned into "turn off the engine—we're not going anywhere!" Yes, within a few miles, traffic had ground to a halt. All the traffic, that is, except for the express lane to our left. There, traffic was still speeding along just fine.

You can imagine what the next hour was like, watching that express lane as we sat motionless. While we tried to make the best of it, thoughts of "If only we had taken that fast lane!" nagged at the back of our minds as cars whizzed by.

And then it hit me. What we were feeling was only an infinitesimal fraction of the dreadful feeling people have if, having come to the end of their lives, they realize that they have taken the wrong road, the broad road Jesus talked about that leads to destruction (Matthew 7:13). What would it be like, I wondered in a new, horrified way, to watch others going down the narrow road to eternal life while I headed toward an eternity of torture with no chance to change my mind or my course? What would that feel like? How badly then would I cry out to be on the other side?

One of the most sobering parables Jesus told dealt with this exact issue.

There was a rich man who lived in luxury. At his gate laid a beggar named Lazarus, covered with sores and longing to eat scraps from the rich man's table. Read this chilling account found in Luke 16:

> The time came when the beggar died and the angels carried him to Abraham's side. The rich man also died and was buried. In Hades, where he was in torment, he looked up and saw Abraham far away, with Lazarus by his side. So he called to him, "Father Abraham, have pity on me and send Lazarus to dip the tip of his finger in water and cool my tongue, because I am in agony in this fire."

> But Abraham replied, "Son, remember that in your lifetime you received your good things, while Lazarus received bad things, but now he is comforted here and you are in agony. And besides all this, between us and you a great chasm has been fixed, so that those who want to go from here to you cannot, nor can anyone cross over from there to us."

> He answered, "Then I beg you, father, send Lazarus to my father's house, for I have five brothers. Let him warn them, so that they will not also come to this place of torment."

Abraham replied, "They have Moses and the Prophets; let them listen to them."

"No, father Abraham," he said, "but if someone from the dead goes to them, they will repent."

He said to him, "If they do not listen to Moses and the Prophets, they will not be convinced even if someone rises from the dead."

The rich man never was allowed to go back and warn his brothers. Nor was he able to go back and make a different choice himself. Having lived apart from Christ, he died apart from Him as well.

Have you ever let your mind really enter into the awfulness of this agonizing scenario? Have you ever tried to visualize those whom you love, or simply the people you come across every day, facing similar, unimaginable regret?

A woman of the harvest lives with this "in Christ/not in Christ" reality at the forefront. Her concern for souls affects how she spends her minutes and her money. It impacts her interactions and her conversations. It informs her goals and her activities. It shapes her hopes and her prayers. Indeed, it permeates her life.

With solemn thoughts about forever,
Rachel

- 45 -
opening our eyes

Do you not say, 'Four months more and then the harvest'?
I tell you, open your eyes and look at the fields!
They are ripe for harvest.
JOHN 4:35

Dear Erin,

Ray Mensah has been a dear friend of ours since we met in Ghana over 15 years ago. He also happens to be one of my missionary heroes. Sacrifice, zeal, integrity, humor, and grace are all words I would use to describe his tireless gospel efforts across his home continent of Africa over the past few decades, impacting thousands.

In 2012, Ray began spearheading an effort to take the gospel to the Komba, an unreached, but very receptive tribe in northern Ghana. Traveling in a sturdy 4x4 pickup truck that had to barrel through flooded areas and carve out roads where there were none, Ray and several coworkers began the work with an arduous survey of over 100 remote villages in order to ascertain where the Komba lived and what their

195

greatest needs were. Along the way, Ray was personally impacted:

> On the very first day of our second survey trip, whilst we worshipped and prayed in the truck driving across the mission fields, I suddenly broke down into tears, weeping profusely. I believe I was overwhelmed once again by the gargantuan needs of the people that I was witnessing in village after village, both spiritual and physical. So many lost people, so many idols, and so many needs…

Somehow, when we come face to face with people's immense spiritual and physical deficiencies, it's hard to stay the same. If our hearts are softened to God, it's hard not to take on His compassion and zeal.

In saying to His disciples, "Open your eyes and look at the fields!" I believe Jesus was actually giving us all a principle by which to live. See, to even begin to grasp the urgency and immensity of the world's spiritual needs, we have to get our eyes off our own little lives and onto the thousands, millions and billions who don't yet know Christ.

Our natural tendency is to think and care about ourselves and whatever is in front of us. If we feed our eyes on catalogs of trendy clothes, we'll think about having trendy clothes. If we obsess about even good things, like healthy food or getting enough exercise, those things will fill our thoughts. But God calls us to set our minds on eternal things (Colossians 3:2). In order to do that, we have to fill our minds with thoughts and images that have to do with eternity—things like souls.

That's what Ray did among the Komba tribe, and his experience birthed an explosive ministry to a people truly "ripe for harvest."

Although I don't do much travel during these days of motherhood, and although Michael and I feel that God wants us building His Kingdom from right where we are in Chicagoland, I try to keep my passion for the entire world stirred and my heart softened by regularly "looking at the fields." Here are just a few of the things I have found helpful.

Get to know internationals. Growing in compassion for people all across the world becomes a lot easier when you actually get to know some of them! Fortunately, in our increasingly transient world, it's not hard to meet people from other cultures. They may be immigrants, refugees, foreign students, or business expatriates. Seek them out! Get to know them and their stories. If they are not part of a large family or international sub-culture, they are often very open to new friendships. Many of them have never been invited into a Christian home or spent time with a Christian family. What an opportunity!

Utilize internet resources. There are some great resources that can put you in touch with the peoples of the world. Visit *www.JoshuaProject.net* and find eye-opening statistics and prayer needs for every people group in the world. Check out *www.Prayercast.com* to see short videos featuring compelling visual imagery, music and prayers for the nations of the world. Or visit *www.GlobalPrayerDigest.org* to read about a different people group each day. Never has it been so easy to see and taste and touch the harvest fields.

Go on a missions trip. Air travel in the last 50 years has revolutionized our ability not only to hear or read about the world from afar, but to go and see it. It's one thing to know that less than 2% of a nation is Christian. It's quite another thing to stand in a sea of people in a crowded foreign marketplace and realize that you may be one of the only Christians for as far as the eye can see.

Visit a local ministry. You don't necessarily have to go globetrotting to get a glimpse of hopelessness. Any number of local Christian ministries can help you come face to face with real needs of real people. It may be a prison, it may be a nursing home, it may be a shelter for teenage mothers. God may use one of these settings to touch your heart and show you a practical way He can use you right where you are.

Read, subscribe and watch. Get your hands on a great missionary biography or story that will help you get to know the people of a certain country and inspire you with what God is doing. Subscribe to missionary newsletters or missions magazines and be regularly encouraged by the larger Body of Christ serving around the globe. Watch or read the news. Find out where people are suffering from an accident, a civil war or a natural disaster. Search out what's going on and be moved to care, to pray, and to take action.

Jesus said, "Where your treasure is, there your heart will be also." Perhaps there is also some truth to the statement, "Where your eyes are, there your thoughts will be also." So go ahead. Look at the fields!

Blessings,
Rachel

- 46 -
offering what we have

"How many loaves do you have?" he asked. "Go and see."
MARK 6:38a

Dear Erin,

While it is crucial to be reminded of the massive needs that exist locally and globally, if you are like me, it is easy to get overwhelmed with the sheer vastness of them as well. Visit *www.OperationWorld.org* and you will find country after country where as many as 98% of the population are "without hope and without God" (Ephesians 2:12). Simply staggering. It's easy to think, "How could I ever help make a dent in that?"

Jesus' disciples knew what it was to come face to face with huge needs. One day, they found themselves at the shore of a lake with thousands of people who had come to see Jesus. Out of His compassion, He started to teach them.

As it got late, the disciples realized that these folks must be hungry. They suggested Jesus send them away so they could go get a bite to eat in a nearby village.

Jesus rather suggested that His *disciples* give them something to eat. They gave Him an, "Are you crazy?" type of answer, explaining how it would cost way too much to feed the crowd. The scope of the need was just too great.

Then Jesus simply said, "How many loaves do you have? Go and see."

He wasn't asking them to spend money they didn't have. He wasn't asking them to meet an enormous need that was beyond their resources. But He *was* interested in what they had.

See, Jesus does not ask for more than we have, but He *does* ask for that. He wants everything that is "us" to be available and surrendered to Him. He wants the rights to our time, our money, our possessions, our husbands, our children, our dreams, our desires, even our reputations. It can be painful for us to let these things go, but how much greater and more useful they become in His hands.

A few years ago we were at a church that had recently lost one of its missionaries as a martyr in Afghanistan. I remember God's still, small voice challenging me with these words, "Rachel, what if you spend your life raising your kids and they all became martyrs, too? Will it be okay with you if that is the end result of all your parenting? Am I worthy of that?" I had the new realization in that moment that if each and every one of our seven children died for the gospel of Christ, it would not be a waste. It would be a costly offering, but not a waste because of Christ's infinite worth and His miraculous power to transform the little we can offer Him into something far more significant.

Whoever gave up their five loaves and two fish as they were with Jesus that day got a firsthand glimpse of this.

Having received the food, Jesus told His disciples to have the people sit down in groups of hundreds and fifties. Giving thanks to God, He broke the loaves and proceeded to have the disciples distribute the miraculously multiplying food to the crowd.

Did you notice how Jesus had the disciples break down the crowd into smaller groups? Big numbers can be helpful in showing us the size of the need, but they can also be intimidating. Sometimes we just need to see one person, one family or one village whose needs we can begin to help meet.

This story also reminds us that when we offer God what we have, He will often "break" it as He prepares to multiply and use it. We might offer Him a gift or talent, and He might seem to "shelve" it, taking away our ability to use it for a season or making us wait for what seems like forever to do so. We might offer Him our womb, and He may not allow us to have the kids we dreamt of raising for Him. Sometimes our "broken loaves" look much different than the original thing we had offered to Him, but if humbly submitted to His refining fire, they can be amazingly molded and multiplied to touch countless lives.

Notice one last thing about the feeding of the 5,000. We can't think that Jesus is going to feed the multitudes without us. We can't think He is going to dismiss the crowds to fend for themselves. He wants them to have "true bread" in abundance and He wants to use you and me to pass it out.

With you in the greatest cause,
Rachel

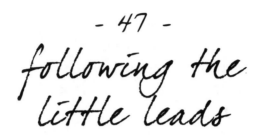

- 47 -
following the little leads

The Spirit told Philip, "Go to that chariot and stay near it." Then Philip ran up to the chariot and heard the man reading Isaiah the prophet. "Do you understand what you are reading?" Philip asked.
ACTS 8:29-30

Dear Erin,

Have you ever had an idea pop into your mind that you knew the Holy Spirit had put there? Maybe it had to do with reaching out to someone through an encouraging word, a gift, a meal or a prayer? Whatever the case, it was something you knew He was asking you to do as an extension of His love.

When our oldest two were young, I used to take them for walks around our neighborhood and we would often see an elderly woman sitting outside her house. We'd stop and talk and eventually became good friends with "Mrs. Katherine."

She would have us in for some of her delicious sour cream cake and let the kids talk with her little parrot in the kitchen.

I enjoyed our visits as well. I loved hearing about Katherine's life, her adult kids and her late husband. I loved looking at her collection of porcelain dolls. And I was inspired to learn that at age 83, she still swam for exercise three times a week!

One night, after we had known her for several months, I put the kids to bed and then felt nudged to walk down and visit Katherine. As she and I sat on her couch talking, the conversation turned to spiritual things. She pulled out her big Catholic Bible to show me. Much like Philip asked the Ethiopian eunuch in Acts 8, I asked Katherine if she understood the things that she read. She responded that although she'd been a faithful church attender all her life, she really didn't understand the Scriptures. "Would you mind if I tried to explain some things?" I asked. "Sure!" she said.

So there I was, with a beautiful opportunity to explain the story of God to this woman with a soft and open heart. I hadn't had to do much to be at this point. I had simply tried to look at Katherine with eternal eyes and walk through doors that God kept opening. He was pursuing her. I was just an instrument of His in the process.

Sometimes reaching out takes sustained forethought and effort. Hudson Taylor didn't end up as a pioneer missionary in China in 1854, for instance, because he followed the next easy step! At other times, however, we just have to be ready to respond to opportunities that God practically places in our laps, requiring just a small step of obedience.

Yes, it might be a "small" step of obedience, but don't let that minimize the word obedience. See, I have also been guilty of not following through on an idea or a nudge that I knew was from Him. Perhaps it was a little inconvenient to carry out the task, and so I rationalized it away. Or maybe I talked myself into thinking it wasn't that urgent. I'd get to it someday.

Recently, however, after utterly failing to seize an easy opportunity God gave me to reach out to a neighbor at Christmastime, I was convicted by this thought: "You know, Rachel, when your kids don't obey you in a timely way, you tell them it's equal to disobedience. It's the same with Me. Your obedience must be timely, or it's not really obedience."

Let us have open eyes and ears for the opportunities God brings our way. In fact, let's pray for just those moments to unfold!

Let us have open eyes and ears for the opportunities God brings our way. In fact, let's pray for just those moments to unfold! And then let's be swift to obey whatever it is He is asking us to do.

Growing with you,
Rachel

- 48 -
service:
a costly endeavor

Then Jesus said to his disciples, "If anyone would come after me, he must deny himself and take up his cross and follow me."
MATTHEW 16:24

Dear Erin,

We need to be wary if serving others for the sake of the gospel never costs us much of anything.

You see, sometimes service can be flat out fun, especially if we are using our spiritual gifts in a way we love or with people we enjoy. At other times, if we are really serving with all of our heart, soul, mind and strength, it will cost us and we'll feel the price dearly.

That's why we're called "living sacrifices." True service often requires giving up things we'd rather keep.

It may cost us time we would rather have spent doing something else. It may cost us money. It may cost us sleep. It may cost us our husbands or our kids (as we have to release them to the Lord in some way), or it may cost us our privacy, as we open up our homes and our lives. Whatever the cost, He sees and receives those labors of love given from the heart as "our spiritual act of worship" (Romans 12:1).

The Apostle Paul knew the painful reality of serving at a cost. Shipwrecks, beatings, imprisonments, hard work, cold, hunger and sleepless nights were just some of the crosses he bore, aside from his "burden for all the churches." He knew what it was to be "poured out" and spent for others (Philippians 2:17).

Jesus had days in ministry that would leave most of us with our tongues hanging out. He got up early. He worked hard. He fasted at times. He knew discomfort. Since a servant is not above his master, should we think that following in His footsteps won't be costly for us as well? If we limit our service to only those things which are enjoyable and convenient, we need to ask ourselves if we are really doing all that He requires of us.

About two years ago, I sensed God was asking me to pay a specific, personal price in order to help bring the gospel to a nation in darkness.

In the following excerpt from my journal, you'll see that He was laying before me a practical self-denial. With my flesh resisting, I had to decide if I was willing to take up my cross and obey even if it cost me.

I'm sharing at our women's Bible study this morning about taking action for the unreached. As I prepare, God is greatly challenging me in my own heart about how much I care and am willing to sacrifice, particularly in regards to North Korea. The Holy Spirit has brought several verses to mind as He has challenged me recently with the thought of fasting for the release of North Korea's captives.

Personally, I've been more concerned about the comfort that my food provides me than I have been about those in North Korea gripped in total bondage and suffering.

If there were ever a wicked and demonic stronghold that could only come out by prayer and fasting, it seems North Korea would qualify (Mark 9:29). The horrors that go on there are almost unimaginable. Whatever is gripping the land is stealing, killing and destroying millions upon millions of lives (John 10:10).

Is God looking for people who will participate with Him in the rescue of these enslaved people, but having trouble finding them (Ezekiel 22:30)? Am I willing to be one or will I keep resisting because I am not willing to deny myself and take up this cross?

I've long prayed for North Korea. Am I also willing to "give myself" in an Isaiah 58 kind of way? Am I willing to work sacrificially to loose the chains of injustice? Will I be among the conquerors on North Korea's behalf when those saved are gathered on the last day? Or will I be ashamed of the "hesitations that hindered" me, as F. Coillard put it?

Will I keep resisting the conviction to fast until Jesus decides to pass over me as one unwilling to serve with

Him in North Korea? Will He have to find someone more caring, more Christlike, more sacrificial than I? "When Jesus calls a man, He bids him come and die," said Bonhoeffer. Have I done all the dying I am willing to do, or am I still the Lord's servant, willing to take up my cross this day?

"Here am I, Lord. Send me!" (Isaiah 6:8). Can I honestly pray this regarding fasting for North Korea? Am I that available and surrendered?

Lord, You are showing me that You want to take me to a new place, a place of suffering and yet a place of power—spiritual power to demolish strongholds.

Do I hate the enemy and what he has done in North Korea enough to be a freedom fighter for her? Military soldiers do very brave things in the fight for earthly justice. Am I willing to be a soldier in the battle of the heavenlies?

Lord, my flesh resists and yet my spirit senses that I would gain in bodily suffering a new nearness with You, an increase of spiritual power over sin and a great satisfaction in obedience.

My flesh and spirit say, "No. Can't there be another way? Lord, take this cup from me." This only shows me that by obeying, I would be able to fellowship with Christ in a new way, walking a road He has walked, not wanting the Father's will, but obeying it anyway.

In the end, I felt led to commit to fasting for North Korea one day a week for a season. Though I had never fasted regularly or for 24 hours at a time before, I was amazed to find Him sustain me physically through the fasting days and draw my heart to stand in the gap for the people of North Korea.

As we make decisions about what Kingdom responsibilities we will take on, we need to be prayerful and careful about not overcommitting or compromising the other roles God has given us. But we also need to make sure we don't say no to everything we don't "feel" like doing. Thankfully, our calling goes far beyond our feelings, as modeled by Jesus when He went to the cross.

We must remind ourselves that there are people who are likely to live and die in hopelessness unless God intervenes in their lives through people like you and me. And if that costs us something, so be it!

With love,
Rachel

- 49 -
the power of intecessory prayer

"What do you want me to do for you?" he asked.
MARK 10:36

Dear Erin,

A millionaire invited his niece to his ranch for the weekend. Before she came, he told himself that he would give her anything she asked for while she was there. But because she didn't know that and thought it would be rude to ask, she didn't request a single thing from him during her stay.

How differently she may have approached things if she knew how willing he was to share with her out of his wealth!

Well guess what? Our God is the wealthiest and most powerful being in the universe! And He's told us that He is willing to do great things in our lives and for His Kingdom if we would just ask Him! Yet how little we seek from Him compared to the powers and treasures at His disposal—especially when it comes to praying for others.

See, we're often very aware of our own needs because we feel them. We live with them. We talk to God about them. But having a mind to ask Him to meet the needs of others—especially their greatest need of knowing Him—takes intentionality, energy and persistence. Yet it is also one of the most strategic and effective ways we can actively participate in making disciples near and far.

Prayer is not a benign force. It's not an optional add-on. And it's not unrelated to what God decides to do. In fact, He has set this up as a law within His Kingdom: "Ask and I will do." As Jack Hayford points out, we can't do anything without Him, but there is also much He will not do without us. It's as if He says to us, "I'll act when you ask."

Like the millionaire, God is waiting for our requests. By taking advantage of His willingness to answer, we can make an eternal impact in ways we might never even know!

Turn every need you become aware of into a prayer. Pray as you watch the news. Pray as you see your neighbors come and go. Pray for unsaved family and friends. Pray for unreached peoples around the world. Pray for missionaries or ministries God puts on your heart. Pray for more harvest workers.

Shoot up random prayers as they come to mind, but also try to pray focused, residual prayers. I try to be in the habit of answering the question Jesus often asked people, "What do you want me to do for you?" (Matthew 20:32; Mark 10:36, 10:51; Luke 18:41) Keep a running, written list of specific things you are asking Him to do in your life, as well as in the lives of others!

And as you pray, be aware that God may lay on your heart an action you can take to be His instrument in answering that prayer. Be willing to be used to accomplish the things you have asked of Him!

Also, be wary of the obstacles to prayer. Here are just a few:

- Praying without faith (James 1:6)
- Praying for selfish reasons (James 4:3)
- Giving up in prayer (Luke 18:1)
- Harboring unconfessed sin (Psalm 66:18)

God has called us to cooperate with Him in His bringing about His Kingdom on earth. Our obedience through prayer is more crucial than we will ever fully know this side of Heaven.

One day, as the Lord was convicting me with these thoughts, I felt like He began to show me just how foolish we are when we don't pray—and how we can't truly be harvest workers without it. I penned these words in my journal:

Lord, You have entrusted to us the souls of men. You have designed it so that Your appeal might be made through us. You have entrusted to us all the power for such a work through Your Spirit.

And yet we don't pray.

The sin of prayerlessness pervades Your people. We are guilty of failing to tap into the richest reservoir in the world. We tap into all sorts of dry and barren wells, but we fail to drink of You.

Woe to you, O Church. You say you are carrying out My

work, but I know nothing of it. I sit and wait as you go and go, and wonder when you'll see. I watch and wonder how you think you can do great things without Me.

All power is Mine, and power you'll receive when My Spirit comes on You. But it won't come apart from seeking My face, no matter what you try to do.

Woe to you, O Church. The world is perishing as we speak, and yet you hardly offer a prayer that isn't based on one of your needs. Have you no heart to intercede as Abraham did for Sodom? Do you not see I listened to him until he was satisfied? And are you satisfied with the billions of souls who, too, will perish in fire? Is that why you don't plead with Me for their salvation? Is that why you've not got time to talk to me—because You are satisfied?

Or is it possibly because you don't believe I'll listen, hear and act? Is it because you think prayer is nothing, a token thing you do that holds no power within itself? It does hold power because that is how I've ordained it to be.

Ask and you will receive. Seek and you will find. Knock and the door will be opened to you (Matthew 6:7).

So what are you asking of Him these days?

Prayerfully,
Rachel

- 50 -
what's your assignment?

*I had not told anyone what my God
had put in my heart to do for Jerusalem.*
NEHEMIAH 2:12

Dear Erin,

I love the handful of Scriptures that let us know God really does give specific assignments and callings to different people. He has certain things on His heart to accomplish and He chooses certain people to carry them out. Let me share just one example.

When Nehemiah, Jewish cupbearer to the king of Persia, heard that his fellow Jews who had returned to Jerusalem after the Babylonian exile were in great trouble, he sat down and wept. The city wall was a heap of ruins. The gates had been burned with fire. Nehemiah mourned, fasted and prayed for the city and its people. In the process, God laid a burden on Nehemiah's heart to be a part of the solution.

After getting permission from the king, Nehemiah returned to the city of his fathers. And then we read this. "I went to Jerusalem, and after staying there three days I set out during the night with a few men. I had not told anyone what my God had put in my heart to do for Jerusalem" (Nehemiah 2:11-12a).

Do you see how Nehemiah states plainly that it was God who had put the strategic task of helping to rebuild the ancient city on his heart?

A few chapters later we read that God continued to move in Nehemiah to carry out the heavenly task of helping to re-establish Jerusalem. "So God put it into my heart to assemble the nobles, the officials and common people for registration by families" (Nehemiah 7:5). Here again, we see that God works through "heart assignments."

Over the years, I have had big and small "heart assignments." Sometimes it has been a quick phone call or note of encouragement to someone. Sometimes it has been a certain dollar amount God puts on Michael's and my heart to give to a ministry or individual. Other times, it has been a long-term project or reaching out through a relationship that has required effort and prayer over the course of several years. Whatever the size or shape of the call, there is something very fulfilling about carrying out Kingdom commissions that you deeply sense God has prepared in advance just for you (Ephesians 2:10)!

So what is it that God has laid on your heart to do? What needs have especially burdened you? Where do you see open doors and feel His pull? As Christian women, there are so many ways we can serve as agents of God's grace! Here are just a few.

Offering Hospitality The well-to-do woman in Shunem provided hospitality to Elisha whenever he came through town. Maybe you have a guest bedroom you can offer from time to time to someone who would be equally blessed. Or perhaps there are people in your life who would love to share a meal around your family dinner table. (2 Kings 4:8-10)

Washing the Feet of the Saints Is there a way you can serve a fellow believer, perhaps in a way that would refresh them, encourage them and better equip them for ministry? (I Timothy 5:9)

Looking After Orphans and Widows Perhaps God is placing on your heart fostering or adopting a child who would be immeasurably blessed to become a part of a Christian home. Is there a widow in your life who would love an occasional phone call, visit or invitation? (James 1:27)

Helping Those in Trouble I know several Christian families who have taken in troubled youth or unwed young mothers. I know of others who actively help the unemployed find jobs, do crisis pregnancy counseling or serve the homeless. Is God calling you to help someone in trouble? (1 Timothy 5:9-10)

Standing in the Gap Has God burdened you to pray for an unsaved friend or family member? A people group or nation? Faithfully and fervently interceding for God to move in a life or in an entire country is significant harvest work. How cool that it can be done from anywhere at anytime! (Ezekiel 22:30)

Reaching Out to the Poor and Needy Are there people in your life whom you can bless through your kindness and generosity? If you don't have many personal connections with people in need, perhaps God will lead you to reach out through your church or a local or global ministry that is serving the poor in Christ's name. (Proverbs 31:20)

Helping to Proclaim the Gospel Both Jesus and the Apostle Paul had women coworkers who helped to meet their needs and do whatever they could to facilitate the gospel going out. Through administrative skills, teaching, writing, praying, cooking, medical work or even hosting a neighborhood Bible study, there are so many ways women can contribute to the gospel going forward! How do you feel called to help? (Luke 8:1-3; Philippians 4:3)

Devoting Yourself to All Kinds of Good Deeds This is a general phrase from Scripture, but I think it points to the fact that there are countless ways that a godly woman can bear spiritual fruit! If we keep the mindset that God wants His saving grace to flow out through us, our eyes will remain peeled for opportunities to be a blessing to people everywhere. (1 Timothy 5:9-10; Titus 3:14)

A woman of the harvest is not marked by a few, isolated good deeds, but by a life that, over time, reflects a heart focused on the things that matter most.

A warm farewell,
Rachel

The Harvest
for personal reflection or group discussion

1. How does the Great Commission affect the way you think or live?

2. How can you grow as an intercessor for the lost?

3. Are there any specific burdens or assignments you feel God has placed on your heart for the purposes of advancing His Kingdom?

Recommended Resources

Operation World: The Definitive Prayer Guide to Every Nation by Jason Mandryk
A book full of an astounding amount of information and statistics related to the state of the gospel in every nation of the world, *Operation World* will equip you to pray with knowledge. It will also open your eyes to just how huge the world's harvest fields are.

www.Prayercast.com
A website full of free, compelling media resources that will equip you to pray for the world. Anchored by videos that highlight individual nations, Prayercast.com is a great resource to help you, your family or your church learn about and pray for the needs of the world.

Radical: Taking Back Your Faith From the American Dream by David Platt
In this best seller, Platt causes us to take a good, hard look at our lives and how we have largely molded Christianity to fit our desires. *Radical* is a stirring challenge to reexamine our lives in light of Christ and the Great Commission.

Don't Waste Your Life by John Piper
This book is a "passionate call to make your life count for eternity." While uncovering the vanity of the way many believers live, Piper encourages his readers to take risks for the sake of the gospel.

Christian Heroes: Then and Now
by Geoff and Janet Benge
Published by Youth With a Mission (YWAM), this wonderful series is filled with biographies of notable and inspiring

missionaries and Christian heroes who have impacted the world. Great for personal reading or for reading aloud to your children, these stories will increase your faith and enlarge your heart for the world.

Living Sacrifice: Willing to Be Whittled As An Arrow by Dr. Helen Roseveare
Having endured both horrific and amazing events as a medical missionary in the Congo, Dr. Roseveare's terrific storytelling and teaching challenges us to give our heart, soul, mind and strength to God for His purposes.

A Chance to Die by Elisabeth Elliott
A beautifully written biography of Irish missionary and author Amy Carmichael, who spent 53 years in India, this book will challenge you to a new understanding of discipleship, surrender and what it really means to love the lost.

Undaunted: Daring To Do What God Calls You To Do by Christine Caine
Against the backdrop of her own painful journey, Caine writes with personal transparency and profound spiritual wisdom. An advocate for victims of human trafficking, Caine inspires the reader to be free from fear to pursue the purposes and calling of God. An excellent blend of narrative and inspiration.

About OneWay Ministries

The mission of OneWay Ministries is to activate God's people to exalt Jesus Christ and advance His gospel to the multitudes. We not only have a passion to see people from around the world come to know Christ, but to see believers beautifully fulfilling their role in that mission. In that pursuit, we focus on the following:

Praise: Inspiring Christ-exalting worship
Prayer: Activating world-changing prayer
Preparation: Exhorting and equipping God's people for Kingdom work
Proclamation: Proclaiming the gospel and establishing churches
Partnership: Linking up with others towards maximum Kingdom fruit

We give birth to various ministries as God leads. Some of our ministries include:

Prayercast.com

Because only God can truly meet the immeasurable needs of the world, one of our primary ministries is to mobilize prayer. Individuals, churches and organizations around the world are using the free, compelling media resources of Prayercast.com to stand in the gap for the lost (Psalm 2:8).

OneWay Africa

With a special passion to mobilize and train African believers for Great Commission work, OneWay Africa aims to reach those who remain least reached on the continent (Mark 16:15).

OneWay Studios
Through the creation of Kingdom-advancing prayer, evangelism, and worship resources, OneWay Studios seeks to equip the Body of Christ and reach the lost (Ephesians 4:12).

BIBLEplus+
Our BIBLEplus+ ministry reaches oral communicators in their heart language by recording and distributing audio Scriptures, testimonies and local worship on solar-powered, handheld media players (Romans 10:17).

Teaching and Worship
Through books, conferences and live worship events, we encourage God's people towards lives of full surrender and involvement in His mission to see all people saved (Romans 12:1-2; 2 Peter 3:9).